Henry Dreyfuss

Industrial Designer

HENRY DREYFUSS

Industrial Designer

THE MAN IN THE BROWN SUIT

Russell Flinchum

Cooper-Hewitt, National Design Museum, Smithsonian Institution & Rizzoli, New York

First published in the United States of America in 1997 by
Rizzoli International Publications, Inc.
300 Park Avenue South, New York NY 10010

Library of Congress Cataloging-in-Publication Data

Flinchum, Russell.
    Henry Dreyfuss, industrial designer : the man in the brown suit /
by Russell Flinchum; introduction by Stanley Marcus; preface by
Dianne Pilgrim.
        p.   cm.
    Includes index.
    ISBN 0-8478-2010-6 (HC)
    1. Dreyfuss, Henry, 1904-   .   2. Industrial designers—United
States—Biography.   3. Design, Industrial—United States—History.
    I. Cooper-Hewitt Museum.   II. Title.
    TS140.D74F55 1997
    745.2´ 092´   96-48155
    [B]—dc21   CIP

Prepared in conjunction with the exhibition "Henry Dreyfuss Directing Design:
The Industrial Designer and His Work, 1929-72" at Cooper-Hewitt, National Design Museum,
Smithsonian Institution, New York, March 18-August 31, 1997.

Designed by Hahn Smith Design, Toronto

Printed and bound in the United States of America

Jacket illustrations: Westclox, Big Ben alarm clock, 1939. Front and back views.
(John Waddell Collection; Photographer, Dennis Cowley)

Frontispiece illustrations: Results of Henry Dreyfuss design, from left to right, top to bottom:
Crane Neuvogue lavatory, 1936; interior, exhibition building for National Supply Co., Tulsa,
Oklahoma, 1959; Hoover Model 010 dry iron with "pancake" dial, 1947; exhibition building for
National Supply Co., Tulsa, Oklahoma, 1959; proposed tractor for Deere & Co., 1959; rendering of
Model 37 transport plane for Consolidated Vultee, 1945; proposed standard typewriter for Royal
Typewriter Co., 1944; Dreyfuss's design team with a model of the Convair Car, 1946; automatic
card-dialing telephone for Bell Telephone Laboratories, 1962; Mod II Picturephone for Bell
Telephone Laboratories, 1967; Trimline telephone for Bell Telephone Laboratories, 1968; Polaroid
Model J33 Land Camera, 1961; thermostat for Honeywell, 1964; Consolidated Vultee Convair Car
in flight, 1947; Hoover Model 305 vacuum cleaner, 1940.

Contents

Mercury locomotive for New York Central Railroad, 1936

Foreword

HENRY DREYFUSS'S RELATIONSHIP TO THIS MUSEUM dates back to 1972, when the industrial designer and his wife, Doris Marks, arranged for the donation of their papers and endowed the Doris and Henry Dreyfuss Memorial Study Center. This gift formed the core of the Museum's Industrial Design Archives, which has grown to include the collections of Donald Deskey, Nathan Horwitt, Ladislav Sutnar, and Don Wallance.

Over the past twenty-five years, works from the Dreyfuss Collection have been studied, published, and exhibited, but the exhibition "Henry Dreyfuss Directing Design: The Industrial Designer and His Work, 1929–72" and the accompanying monograph are the first to provide a cohesive picture of Dreyfuss's life and career.

This first major retrospective of the work of Henry Dreyfuss comes as the third exhibition in a series focusing on the design process. "Mechanical Brides: Women and Machines from Office to Home" (1993) explored the often complex relationship between women and industrial design. "Packaging the New: Design and the American Consumer, 1925–1975" (1994) investigated the role of design in the evolution of consumer culture. "Henry Dreyfuss Directing Design" examines the work of one particular and accomplished industrial designer in the context of specific clients and commissions. The Dreyfuss Collection has provided a wealth of information and material that helped us explore the process of design through case studies of designer and client relationships.

I am indebted to Stanley Marcus for writing the introduction to this book. He provided insight into the life and career of his longtime friend. Indeed, we have benefited from the many personal reminiscences of Henry Dreyfuss's friends and colleagues, making the man in the brown suit a *person*, rather than folklore. As the first Peter Krueger/Christie's Fellow at the National Design Museum in 1989–90, author Russell Flinchum began his in-depth study of Henry Dreyfuss. Over the past seven years his diligence and determination have allowed him to plumb the depths of the collection, explore the context of this body of material, and synthesize it with scholarly care. I am grateful to Russell for his grace, patience, and good humor. His knowledge of design in general and Henry Dreyfuss in particular is evident in the exhibition and this publication, both of which will make a lasting contribution to our understanding of design history. Kathleen Luhrs deserves special mention and thanks for her work as editor of this book. We gratefully acknowledge support for this publication from the Andrew W. Mellon Foundation Challenge Grant Endowment Fund.

Design influences many aspects of our lives. It affects individual objects and entire communities. It is the thread that connects specific needs with actual solutions. Henry Dreyfuss's legacy, the hundreds of sketches, notes, and clippings preserved at the National Design Museum, illustrates the fertile and sensitive mind of a man whose work continues to be a presence in our daily lives. For client, consumer, and designer, Henry Dreyfuss's story is a true example of the process, products, and importance of design.

Dianne H. Pilgrim, Director
Cooper-Hewitt, National Design Museum

Tap-Lite light switch for Honeywell, 1957

Preface

INTEGRITY IS THE WORD USED MOST OFTEN by Henry Dreyfuss's contemporaries to describe his conception of design, and it is a word often associated with the man himself. Many people, meeting Dreyfuss for the first time, assumed that he had always been "all of one piece," as designer George Nelson defined him in a tribute.[1] No doubt this was the impression that Dreyfuss conveyed. It is my contention, however, that beneath this businesslike exterior was a man who saw himself as an artist, who was deeply concerned with his own place in history and sensitive to the compromises he had to make to realize success. He was a classic overachiever, demanding much of himself and of others; yet he possessed a gentleness and a sense of irony, almost playing the role of "Henry Dreyfuss."

Dreyfuss was "a towering figure" to Raymond Spilman, an industrial designer and biographer of others in the field.[2] Arthur N. BecVar, another member of this generation of designers, recalled these salient points about Dreyfuss:

> His personality was warm and friendly — informal but convincing. It pervaded his relations with management, marketing, engineers and staff designers. He respected the viewpoints of each individual. His unique personality along with his fine physical bearing plus a good knowledge of business fundamentals separated him from many design visionaries. He was an astute businessman as well as a skilled designer.

A few days later, BecVar added:

> Dreyfuss was a gentleman in his business dealings — honest and fair — reflected in his designs.
>
> He dressed in a conservative business suit — always "Brown" — which he must have felt visually reflected his business approach. Not flamboyant — which was the case of some designers at that time.[3]

These estimations come from fellow experts who also knew Dreyfuss from the American Society of Industrial Designers, their professional organization.[4] They knew him during a period when industrial design was at its zenith and enjoyed its highest level of popular esteem — the late 1930s to the late 1950s.[5] To these men and many others, Henry Dreyfuss was "a visionary." He was also eminently practical, responsible, moral, and financially successful. He mediated between manufacturers and consumers to their mutual benefit, and to his own. His is an American success story. The present narrative continues to pose the question of what drove him — it is a first attempt to address what in fact may be an unanswerable question, or one for which the answer is surprisingly simple.

Dreyfuss's artistic development and career have merited a study for a number of years. Although general histories of industrial design in the United States, such as Jeffrey L. Meikle's *Twentieth Century Limited* and Arthur Pulos's *American Design Ethic* and its companion volume, *The American Design Adventure*, have identified Dreyfuss as an exceptionally important figure, no monograph on Dreyfuss's life and work has been written until now.[6] Meikle's book outlines Dreyfuss's early life and identifies most of the major events in his personal evolution, drawing attention, for example, to the influence on his character of the New York Society for Ethical Culture and its school. Pulos's work acknowledges the Dreyfuss firm's crucial role in the professionalization of industrial design and Dreyfuss's part in the leadership of the Society of Industrial Designers and its successor organizations. No critique has succeeded, however, in setting Dreyfuss apart from his contemporaries in terms of the visual qualities of his work. Nor has his manner of managing his firm or the identification of important members of his office constituted part of most previous writers' accounts. No source deals comprehensively with Dreyfuss's many statements about the role of the industrial designer and the practical aspects of creating a successful mass-produced design. Too often, Dreyfuss has taken a back seat to Raymond Loewy as America's most famous industrial designer. There has been no retrospective exhibition of Dreyfuss's work since 1971.[7] Academic neglect of his legacy stands in stark contrast to the tremendous respect accorded him by his fellow designers.

Widely admired by his contemporaries, Dreyfuss is regarded as a major historical figure by industrial designers today. Yet his basic messages about the profession and his role in its development have been diluted, and in some cases misunderstood, by authors working from secondhand accounts. It is important that designers and those who study the history of design today understand the moral imperatives that were first stated by Dreyfuss, analyze the aims he set forth as one of the creators of the industrial design profession, and look for examples of how one of the quintessential practitioners in the field ran a successful design enterprise.[8]

The foundation for this book is the Henry Dreyfuss Collection, part of the Industrial Design Archives in the library of Cooper-Hewitt, National Design Museum, Smithsonian Institution. The Dreyfuss Collection, as it will be referred to throughout this book, contains numerous clippings, photographs, photostatic copies, and approximately a dozen presentation books relating to specific commissions. Correspondence and written material pertaining to the development of projects is largely absent. Dreyfuss was highly selective when he culled through the tremendous range of projects he worked on between 1923 and 1972. The work he executed toward the end of his career dominates the collection. For example, the files and data bank assembled for the creation of his *Symbol Sourcebook* (1972) exist completely intact, while the file for a major client, Bell Telephone Laboratories, contains only a handful of photographs and press releases from the late 1960s. Perhaps Dreyfuss expected the clients to maintain such files. Luckily, microfilm records kept by his office provide an almost complete record of its output up to 1972. Nearly four hundred reels of microfilm were donated to the library in 1991 by Henry Dreyfuss Associates (as the firm was renamed in 1969).[9] While only poor-quality reproductions can be retrieved from the microfilm, this resource is crucial to understanding the extant visual material. The microfilm records allow us to see when a particular sketch was executed and its place in a project's development.

Interviews with contemporaries, co-workers, and family members have been invaluable in framing this initial survey of Dreyfuss's life and work. A great deal remains to be done in terms of defining the roles of various people within the firm. More important, perhaps, is making a new generation aware of the man whose significance is not merely historical. The example of Henry Dreyfuss's life illustrates that, although difficult, the realization of personal success while serving society's needs is indeed possible. We can take heart that this man, a model of probity, was able to negotiate the treacherous waters of big business and see so many of his hopes for his fellow citizens realized.

NOTES

1. George Nelson, in "Henry Dreyfuss, 1904–1972," *Industrial Design* 20 (March 1973), 43.

2. Raymond Spilman, letter to author, November 21, 1991.

3. BecVar was the manager of industrial design for General Electric Company when he became acquainted with Dreyfuss. Arthur N. BecVar, letters to author, October 7 and 9, 1992.

4. BecVar and Spilman are past presidents of the American Society of Industrial Designers (ASID), serving in 1955 and 1960, respectively. The ASID was the successor to the Society of Industrial Designers, established in 1944, and the immediate predecessor to the Industrial Designers Society of America, the name of the organization today.

5. Indicative of the growing recognition of the profession is a scene in Alfred Hitchcock's movie *North by Northwest* (1959). Seated in the Dreyfuss-designed dining car of the 1948 version of the 20th Century Limited train, the protagonist, played by Cary Grant, asks the heroine, played by Eva Marie Saint, what she does for a living. "I'm an industrial designer" is her reply.

6. Jeffrey L. Meikle, *Twentieth Century Limited: Industrial Design in the United States, 1925-1939* (Philadelphia: Temple University Press, 1979); Arthur Pulos, *American Design Ethic: A History of Industrial Design to 1940* (Cambridge, Mass.: MIT Press, 1983) and Pulos, *The American Design Adventure, 1940–1975* (Cambridge, Mass.: MIT Press, 1988).

7. "Designing for People: Retrospective Exhibit of the Works of Henry Dreyfuss," Hall's Exhibition Gallery, Kansas City, Missouri, June 3–July 10, 1971. "Henry Dreyfuss Directing Design," guest-curated by the author, opened at the National Design Museum in the spring of 1997.

8. "This year [1959] industry will spend $500 million to spruce up product looks, product sales appeal. How much of that half billion Dreyfuss himself will snag, nobody but closemouthed (about money) Henry Dreyfuss and the Treasury will know. One certainty: Dreyfuss will be the best-paid designer per working employee in the U.S. Only Loewy Associates' 145-man staff (compared with Dreyfuss' force of 30) will gross more — about $3 million this year." "Machine Age Artist," *Forbes* 67 (May 1, 1951), 18–20. Dreyfuss was featured on the cover of this issue. See also Seymour Freedgood, "Odd Business This Industrial Design," *Fortune* 59 (February 1959), 201, for a listing of the twenty largest industrial design firms in the United States at that time.

9. From its founding in 1929 through 1966, the firm was known simply as Henry Dreyfuss. It was renamed Henry Dreyfuss and Associates about 1967. Dreyfuss left the firm on January 1, 1969. He had sketches, renderings, photographs, and a few written documents (those that directly related to the visual materials) dating back to 1929 microfilmed in 1948. It appears that the bulk of the originals were then destroyed. Work continued to be microfilmed after its completion until 1972.

Washing Machine for Hoover Ltd. (England), 1950

Acknowledgments

ONE OF THE DELIGHTS OF RESEARCHING the life and work of Henry Dreyfuss has been the readiness of his family, friends, and co-workers to share their recollections with me. I could not have begun to understand Henry Dreyfuss without the help of John Dreyfuss and Gail Dreyfuss Wilson, his surviving children. Rita Hart, Bill Purcell, Jim Conner, Niels Diffrient, and Don Genaro of the Henry Dreyfuss office provided insights into his character and working methods that were invaluable. Jim Ryan, Jack McGarvey, and Gordon Sylvester of Henry Dreyfuss Associates have been constantly supportive of my efforts, and my discussions with Bill Wenger and the late Alvin Tilley were essential to formulating an approach to the history of human factors in industrial design (a history that has yet to be written). John Hamilton and Juanita Alexander responded to my many requests for material. Strother MacMinn's and John Bruce's recollections of the office and its personnel in the period following World War II brought them to life for me; Don Holden and Jack Lowery did the same for the late 1950s and 1960s. Edward Larrabee Barnes, Mildred Constantine, Bill Hewitt, and Stanley Marcus shared personal reminiscences of their close friends Henry Dreyfuss and Doris Marks. Clifford Goldsmith, Frederick P. Rose, and many others who knew Dreyfuss professionally added a dimension to my portrait that would otherwise be missing. Any factual errors to be found here, however, remain my own.

The Smithsonian Special Exhibition Fund made "Henry Dreyfuss Directing Design" a reality. Funding from the Hallmark Corporate Foundation came at a critical juncture in our project, and Jeannette Lee, Jon Henderson, and Bill Tinker showed an interest in my work that was greatly appreciated. Honeywell also provided substantial funding; Mike Stapp's enthusiasm was unquenchable, and Nina Hammon's assistance with historical materials helped put the story in order; Ann Drake and her associates enabled us to finalize our story. Jim Odom, working first for Dreyfuss and then for Honeywell, was an invaluable informant and rediscovered material that clarified my account of the "round" thermostat's development. Herbert Bissell's account of the thermostat was critical to obtaining a balanced view of Dreyfuss's involvement in the design process. Worldesign Foundation also supported our efforts, and we have Don Rorke and Robert Schwartz to thank for their help. The Crane Foundation, the National Endowment for the Arts, Furthermore, a program of the J. M. Kaplan Fund, the Stanley and Linda Marcus Foundation, Mr. Niels Diffrient, Knoll International, and the New York State Council on the Arts were kind enough to lend support as well. Finally, the Horace W. Goldsmith Foundation "put us over the top" in our fundraising efforts. The book was funded in part through the Andrew W. Mellon Foundation Challenge Grant Endowment Fund.

The archivists of former Dreyfuss clients were all generous with their time: Les Stegh at Deere & Co.; Sheldon Hochheiser, Tracy Quindlan, Judy Pollack, Ed Eckert, and Bill Heffernen at AT&T; Jacquelyn Love at the Hoover Co.; and Stacy Krammis at the Hoover Historical Society. At Polaroid, Nasrin Rohani helped me discover numerous early models of cameras with which the Dreyfuss office was involved. H. Lansing

Vail of the New York Central Historical Society made it possible for us to document the 20th Century Limited and other railroad work. Special thanks go to Bernard Crystal, Barbara Michaels, and Judith Rich for their help with materials from the Society for Ethical Culture/Fieldston School Archives.

At the Graduate School and University Center of the City University of New York, where this work began, I owe a particular debt of thanks to Professor Marlene Park, who has shown tremendous enthusiasm for my interest in industrial design and patience with the fits and starts that characterized my writing about Henry Dreyfuss's career. Professor Rosemarie Haag Bletter offered critical insights that were particularly helpful regarding European developments during this same period. Rose-Carol Washton-Long, executive officer of the Ph.D. Program in Art History, has supported my desire to specialize in the history of industrial design. The contributions that other teachers made and the encouragement of my colleagues can only be noted here: suffice it to say that the largest part of my education has taken place outside of the classroom. I am grateful for scholarships from the Samuel H. Kress Foundation and the CUNY Department of Art History. While it has been over a decade since I studied with him, I feel it is essential to acknowledge Edson Armi, who challenged me as a freshman at the University of North Carolina and continued to goad me as I left English literature for art history. His belief—that the history of industrial design in the United States was being overlooked, and that many writers failed to appreciate the subtleties of Henry Dreyfuss's aesthetic—drove me on. Without his demands for explanations none of this would have seemed necessary.

In the production of this book, I have been particularly fortunate to work with an outstanding group of people at Rizzoli International Publications: David Morton, Elizabeth White, Megan McFarland, and Tim Terhune have all dealt graciously with the time constraints placed on this project. Meetings with them led to working with the designers Alison Hahn and Nigel Smith, who have shown a tremendous sensitivity to the material they were given and to the particular challenges that photographic documentation of Dreyfuss's career posed. I could not have asked for a happier relationship with the people who made my first book a reality.

At the National Design Museum, where I have been made to feel at home for the last six years, it seems almost impossible to thank anyone without thanking everyone. Nonetheless, in addition to my gratitude to the entire staff, I want to thank particularly Stephen Van Dyk, Chief Librarian at the Museum, who has been interested and helpful in my work with the Dreyfuss Collection; he has always made room for me to work in his domain even when space was at a premium. The staff of the Drawings and Prints Department has kindly responded to my many and varied requests for assistance with the "fine art" elements of Dreyfuss's bequest. The determination of Susan Yelavich, Assistant Director for Public Programs, to make the Dreyfuss exhibition a reality has translated into the wherewithal to do so; and the attention of Linda Dunne, Assistant Director for Administration, to the financial and physical aspects of the exhibition has been constant.

There are four people who deserve special recognition for their support. The first is Dianne Pilgrim, Director of the National Design Museum, who has been constantly supportive of my work on Henry Dreyfuss. Dianne's personal example and her deep convictions about the importance of design have been critical to me throughout this project. Nancy Aakre, the Museum's editor, was always convinced of the validity of this work and "made it happen." Kathleen Luhrs, editor for this project, has been nothing short of a godsend; her patience with me and willingness to work through my sometimes vague pronouncements have been nothing short of remarkable. I thank my wife, Janis, who doesn't believe me when I say that this book never would have happened without her. Sorry dear, it's the truth.

Finally, this book is written in memory of my father, who made all things possible for me.

Other individuals I am indebted to are listed below, and, where appropriate, the institutions they represent.

Tammis Groft, Wesley Balla, Carolyn Wilson, Susan Karp, Albany Institute of History & Art; Donald Albrecht; Stephen Cassell, Thomas Jenkinson, Adam Yarinsky, ARO (Architecture Research Office); Arthur N. BecVar; Eric and Nanette Brill; Amy Chen; the late Richard J. Cook, Sr.; Dennis Cowley; Donald Dailey; Charles W. ("Chuck") Pelly, Designworks/USA; Jack Doern; Michelle D'Souza; Arthur Dubin; Linda Edgerly; Frank Friday, Friday Associates International; Aline Gaughan; Bud Gibbs; Mildred Morton Gilbert; Walter Gips; Katherine and Clifford Goldsmith; Leonard Gordy; Glenn Porter, Hagley Museum; John M. Anderson, Hall of History Foundation; Kim Healey; Mary C. Henderson; Mrs. H. Earl Hoover and Mr. H. E. ("Bud") Hoover II; Mrs. Ann Hose; Alexander Isley Design; Larry Jones; Bill Kaper; Shelley Nickles Kaplan; Linda King; Peter Lawrence, Corporate Design Foundation; Randy Leffingwell; Eugene Levy; Marisha Battle, Library of Congress; Dick Luckin; Wally Aikens, Luminator Aircraft Products; David Revere McFadden; Nic Maffei; Liz Marcus; Jeffrey Meikle; Ralph Meyer; Melissa Miller, Henry Ransom Humanities Research Center, University of Texas; Penny Becker, Minnesota Inventors Congress; Rachael Mullins; the late C. Stowe Myers; Ruth Nathan; Guy Nawy; L. Susan Tolbert, National Museum of American History; John Kovach, National New York Central Railroad Museum; Patricia Tomes, National Watch & Clock Museum; Charlie Smith; John Okolowicz; Bernice A. "Bunny" Cramer, PAOS Boston Inc.; Burt Pittler; Arthur Pulos; James Reeler; Elizabeth Reese; Roger Mark Singer; Raymond Spilman; Todd Stockwell; Cynthia Swank; Walter Dorwin Teague, Jr.; United Scenic Artists Local 829; Sally Clarke, University of Texas; John Waddell; Griselda Warr; Karen Nitkin, Write Stuff Syndicate.

Introduction

HENRY DREYFUSS (1904–1972)

by Stanley Marcus

I T WAS MY GOOD FORTUNE to have been in Paris in 1925 and to have had the opportunity to attend the Exposition Internationale des Arts Décoratifs et Industriels Modernes. It had a profound effect on me, increasing my interest in contemporary architecture and especially in the group of designers who were pioneering the new profession of industrial design. I quickly learned that the design leaders in the United States were Walter Teague, Raymond Loewy, and Henry Dreyfuss.

I had met Loewy shortly after he had arrived in New York. I was introduced to Teague, whom I found to be somewhat stiff and disinterested in someone not likely to be a potential client. But the one to whom I was particularly attracted was Henry Dreyfuss, who had been described in advance as a warm, friendly person.

By chance I was introduced to him and his wife, Doris, at the intermission of a theater performance in New York. We had a brief conversation, and they invited us for dinner the following evening. This was the beginning of an enduring friendship that lasted until the time of their deaths on October 5, 1972.

We shared a community of interests, ranging from retailing to bookmaking, and from education to fashion. Actually, I never found a subject that didn't interest him. We both had children of the same ages and genders, which tightened our bond.

Dreyfuss was an extraordinary human being who loved life in all of its aspects. He was a talented designer without any of the temperamental baggage that so often accompanies that vocation. He had respect for his fellow humans, and his ear was always available to anybody who had an idea or a cause to discuss.

His generosity to his friends became legendary; he had the ability to give time and attention to matters of interest to them. He was never too busy to be generous with his time and his ideas.

Deere Day in Dallas, 1960. Standing left to right: William Hewitt, Henry Dreyfuss, Stanley Marcus, and Patricia Wiman Hewitt.

Very early in our relationship, he became interested in a project that I was working on at Neiman Marcus. For several years we had been producing a fashion show in which we animated a whole series of Christmas gifts by showing them on walking mannequins. Henry, who possessed a native merchandising sense, was fascinated with the idea and began to develop a whole series of runway concepts. At dinner at his favorite corner table in the Oak Room at the Plaza Hotel, we would sit for several hours doodling scores of ways in which a model could wear a skirt made of men's neckties or be transformed into a walking perfume bottle. This professional assistance enhanced our Christmas extravaganza immeasurably. Suddenly we had the "Broadway touch"; Henry never tired of this extracurricular activity, and he frequently called me from New York to tell me of a new idea that had come to his mind. All of his contributions were for free.

He loved to shop stores and boutiques as much as I did, so on Sundays when all the Fifth Avenue places were closed we would go to Chinatown or the Lower East Side where retailing was in full swing. His wife, Doris, hated to shop, and as a matter of fact returned the many fanciful gifts that Henry was perpetually trying to give her. It was

Henry Dreyfuss in his California office. He is sketching his cartoon figure Gladys.

only the bitter cold of a New York winter that made her reluctantly accept a mink coat that Henry wanted her to have. She wore it with reluctance.

When he decided to move their home to Pasadena where he thought that Doris could escape the New York allergies that were plaguing her, he realized that he would be complicating his life radically. He maintained his design office in Manhattan with the bulk of its staff to continue to serve his clients, most of whom were located on the East Coast. He arranged to have guaranteed living accommodations at the Plaza, directly across the street from his office where he kept a full wardrobe, and he proceeded to commute every few weeks from Pasadena.

Henry had the ability to simplify his life in small ways. He never experimented with hotels, satisfied as he was with the Plaza; he wore only one color in suits — brown. That meant that he never had to make a decision as to what color suit or shoes to put on or which tie to select, for the answer was always brown. Normally he ate at one of two restaurants, either "21" or at his corner table in the Plaza's Oak Room, which bore a plaque of dedication to the legendary George M. Cohan.

Henry was born poor in New York and ended up rich in friendships around the world. He did not go to college, but he never permitted that fact from keeping him from becoming an educated man with a depth of knowledge in all fields. His clients were some of the wealthiest companies in the nation, but he also helped blacklisted writers in the McCarthy era. He married Doris Marks, who came from a wealthy family, and she became his business manager, handling all of his contracts and financial matters. Business details never really interested him, and he was perfectly content to leave them to his wife.

He accompanied her to the grave when her cancer became too painful for her to want to continue to live. No greater devotion has any man shown to the woman he loved.

The most elegant appraisal of Henry came from his son, John, who said very simply, "My father was the most honest and ethical man I ever knew. He was always on the side of integrity."

Stanley Marcus is a retail executive best known for his major innovations at the Dallas-based speciality store Neiman Marcus, where he has served in various executive positions since 1926 and of which he is presently chairman emeritus. Born in 1905, he has long been active in civic and cultural organizations in his native Dallas and has received several European honors, including the Chevalier of the French Legion of Honor, the Great Cross of Austria, and the Star of Italian Solidarity. Mr Marcus's articles on retailing and business have been published in Fortune, *the* Atlantic Monthly, *and the* Saturday Evening Post, *among other magazines, and he is the author of four books:* Minding the Store *(1974),* Quest for the Best *(1979),* His & Hers: The Fantasy World of the Neiman-Marcus Catalogue *(1982), and* The Viewpoints of Stanley Marcus: A Ten-Year Perspective *(1995). With William Hewitt, he published privately a collection of drawings of Henry Dreyfuss's cartoon character Gladys. His personal interests have ranged from fine printing and the publication of miniature books to the public affairs organization Common Cause.*

Trimline telephone for Bell Telephone Laboratories, 1968

BECOMING HENRY DREYFUSS

THOUGH HENRY DREYFUSS WAS READY and willing to discuss both professional and theoretical design issues with interviewers, he was less willing to disclose the essentials of his early life and family background. Indeed, the normally gregarious Dreyfuss was tight-lipped on the subject of his childhood and schooling. His autobiography, *Designing for People,* deals only with his life from the late 1920s. The details of his early years must therefore be pieced together from a number of sources. This chapter will put those pieces together, chronologically, from his birth through the establishment of the industrial design firm that bore his name.

The most important source of information for Dreyfuss's life is the record he kept of his professional career, referred to in his office as the "Brown Book" but titled by Dreyfuss "A Record of Personal and Business Vital Statistics." Crucial for his early years is a brief manuscript entitled "The little I know about my family background," which he wrote to his son, John, before his death in 1972.[1] From these two sources the following information can be established.

Henry Dreyfuss's ancestry is not unlike that of many European immigrants to the United States during the decades before the turn of the century. It is a story of hardships, tragedies, close family ties, and eventual triumphs. Moritz Dreyfuss and Sophie Oppenheimer, Dreyfuss's paternal grandparents, were married on January 26, 1873, in Mannheim, Germany. Immediately afterwards they emigrated to New York, where they had four children: Henry and Carrie, both of whom died in an epidemic, Louis (Henry Dreyfuss's father), and Josie. Moritz Dreyfuss founded a business, M. Dreyfuss & Son, at 131 West 23rd Street in New York, which supplied fine materials for theatrical costumes and scenery. Louis Dreyfuss (1878–1915) worked as a tailor and was connected to his father's store. On June 4, 1903, Louis married Elsie Gorge (1880–1937), who came to the United States with her mother, Charlotte Jelenko (later Gorge). Elsie's siblings were Maurice, Malvina, Sigmund, and Hugo Gorge.

At the time of Henry's birth (March 2, 1904), Louis and Elsie Dreyfuss lived in Manhattan with Moritz and Sophie Dreyfuss at the northeast corner of 127th Street and Seventh Avenue. They moved to Bensonhurst in Brooklyn, where Henry's brother, Arnold, was born on February 20, 1909. Soon afterward they returned to Manhattan and again lived with Louis's parents, now at 363 West 120th Street. Henry attended Public School 157 from September 1910 through October 1914. It was about this time that his grandparents died and his father contracted tuberculosis. For the sake of Louis's health, the family moved to Saranac Lake, New York. Henry Dreyfuss remembered over sixty years later that "*it was cold*" [his emphasis]. Within two months, the family moved yet again, to Morristown, New Jersey, where Mrs. Dreyfuss's sister Malvina Gorge had rented a house. Louis Dreyfuss died the night of their arrival in Morristown.

Elsie Dreyfuss and her two young sons returned to Manhattan around January or February 1915, where they lived at Bass's Boarding House at 147 West 118th Street. Henry attended Public School 10 from February 1915 until June 1918. He delivered

Store window advertising *Designing for People*, 1955, Dreyfuss Collection. Objects include left to right: scale model Deere & Co. harvester, Model 500 desk set telephone, plate from the Persian Room, Honeywell Round thermostat, scale model Deere crawler-type tractor.

suits for a tailor and painted signs to help support the family. In later years he said little about this stage of his life to either friends or family; it was probably a period of hardship for all three. His younger brother, Arnold, had contracted St. Vitus's Dance and suffered from a number of other debilitating illnesses. Yet Henry recalled elements of his childhood with a light touch: to one interviewer he recounted an episode in which he trimmed his mother's hat with fresh vegetables he had raided from the icebox.[2]

Henry Dreyfuss's first break came during 1919–20, when he spent the year at Townsend Harris High School. An instructor whom he did not name gave him a grade of 100 percent on the art section of the state regents' examination; Dreyfuss recalled that the Board of Regents in Albany returned the paper with a grade of 98 percent and the statement that nobody could be perfect in the subject. Henry left school in disgust shortly thereafter and thought that his formal education was over. To his surprise, his instructor had contacted the New York Society for Ethical Culture and apparently told them of Henry's great promise. The Society responded with an offer of a two-year scholarship to its private school.

The Ethical Culture movement, founded in 1876 by Felix Adler, was dedicated to affecting positive moral practice in society, ranging in scope from personal to international relations, without relying on belief in a deity as a means to this end.[3] The school that the New York Society operated tried to inculcate the values of group cooperation, individual responsibility, and progressive social values through classes devoted to discussion of ethics in contemporary society (these were in addition to instruction in more traditional academic subjects).[4] Dreyfuss's education in the prevocational art program, however, is important with respect to his formal development. Contemporary with Dreyfuss's arrival were some major changes in the school's instructional focus. Students would focus on training in fine art and craft as they related to handicraft and industrial production in the contemporary environment.

Dreyfuss attended the Ethical Culture Society's Arts High School from September of 1920 until June of 1922. This seminal period for his development as a designer came just as the school inaugurated a "tracking" program for high-school juniors and seniors that was termed prevocational. Under this program, students could elect to join a prevocational department in art, teacher training, or college preparatory, or remain in the regular program. Although these programs were normally reserved for students who had been in the school's programs for the first two years, Dreyfuss was an exception in that he was admitted and enrolled only during the two final years.

The prevocational art program's curriculum was a wide-ranging course of study that exposed students to diverse cultures and historical periods. This highly structured course of study not only taught students the techniques artists employed and surveyed art history, but also covered chemistry and physics as they related to craftsmanship. Literature served as a source for artistic inspiration; history classes were oriented toward the knowledge of the great cultures of the past, with at least an hour each week spent at the Metropolitan Museum of Art inspecting and copying works of art from all periods. The program's catalogue stated boldly, "Nothing else than a new conception of culture is involved in this plan."[5] The study of French and German was also required.

This education prepared Dreyfuss to become the model of the "cultivated man," whose interests ranged from pre-Columbian sculpture to classical music. He made friends in numerous areas of artistic endeavor, with Theodor Geisel (Dr. Seuss) of children's literature at one end of the spectrum and Vincent Price, the leading actor of legendary horror films, at the other. Works by Ben Shahn and Isamu Noguchi were displayed in the Dreyfuss household. While he may have regretted his lack of a college education in later years, his intellectual pursuits never abated. Toward the end of his life he attempted to form reasoned opinions about the nature of creativity and the possibility of universal communication. Henry Dreyfuss was a generalist in the most positive sense of the term. The final years of his formal education had a strong influence on the shape of his lifelong inquisitiveness.

The curriculum at the Ethical Culture school was not restricted to the fine arts. Included were "metal crafts and industrial arts," and the "study of low relief, cameo, intaglio." "Modern industrial applications of above materials" were studied, as were lettering and bookbinding, "design and execution of projects in ceramics" (as well as sculptural work in clay), and elementary architecture and its "application to industrial problems of to-day: textiles, metals, crafts, etc."[6] In line with the Ethical Culture school's mission of helping individuals reach self-actualization, the program was an ambitious compromise between training the student to be a fine artist — well-versed in a craft — and exposing him or her to enough technical knowledge to earn a living outside of the fine arts. The Ethical Culture school also provided a place of refuge and respite for Dreyfuss, and a nurturing environment that encouraged his development in numerous ways.

Personal examples were as important to Dreyfuss's education as the program of study. At the school, Dreyfuss met two adults who would provide, respectively, moral and practical guidance. Teacher and administrator John Lovejoy Elliott gave him the

moral grounding to build working relationships with other people and to understand unique needs. His English teacher, Emma Mueden, gave him the practical knowledge of how to create a stage production (and later introduced him to his future wife). Together Elliott and Miss Mueden awakened Dreyfuss's interest and set high standards that he sought to fulfill. Elliott was, at the time of his death in 1942, the senior leader of the New York Society for Ethical Culture, having succeeded founder Felix Adler. Dreyfuss credited Elliott with giving him "purpose and direction" in life.[7] The extent of his contact with Elliott is speculative. Most likely, Elliott was Dreyfuss's teacher for the ethics course that was mandatory for students. Many of Dreyfuss's notions of what constituted good design can certainly be traced to Elliott's ideas and the Aristotelian tradition of what constitutes a life well lived. In some respects, Dreyfuss saw the role of the industrial designer as a mediator of public taste between the manufacturer and the consumer, analogous to that of the role that Elliott played as a teacher of public values and responsibility between society and citizen.[8]

How Elliott found his calling is worth noting, in light of Dreyfuss's comment that he gave him "purpose and direction," and demonstrates that one generation can act as torchbearer for the next. While a freshman at Cornell, Elliott attended a lecture by Adler that dealt with the possibility of employing oneself in the field of ethical leadership. The son of reform-minded parents, Elliott was moved to devote his life and his talents to the causes that Adler advocated. Like Adler, Elliott studied in Germany, where he earned a doctorate in philosophy at the University of Halle. He returned to the United States and became Adler's assistant and a teacher of ethics at the schools of the New York Society for Ethical Culture. In contrast with Felix Adler's more reserved bearing, Elliott related easily to students.

Top: John Lovejoy Elliott was one of the seminal influences on Dreyfuss. The principal administrator of the Society for Ethical Culture in New York for many years, Elliott, in both bearing and accomplishments, was important to a young man who had lost his father at age eleven.

Bottom: Emma Mueden affected young Dreyfuss with her sense of imagination and can-do attitude. A lifelong friend of Dreyfuss and his wife, Doris Marks, Miss Mueden was responsible for bringing them together for the first time.

To a large extent, Dreyfuss seems to have modeled himself after Elliott, especially in his sense of self-imposed restraint. Like Elliott, he faced what many people felt was an insurmountable task — the elevation of public standards through personal action. Both tried to win others over to their point of view through example and rational persuasion.[9]

Emma Mueden was the other, very different, formative influence on Dreyfuss during the last two years of his education. An English teacher and dean of girls, she was also in charge of all school plays and pageants, which were considered an integral part of the students' education. These productions, referred to as festivals, involved most of the student body and had a didactic purpose, stressing historical figures and events. Perhaps because of his family's experience in the costume business, Dreyfuss became the student responsible for festival settings and costumes during his two years at the school.

Miss Mueden was one of the mainstays of the school and taught there from about 1903 until her retirement in 1951. She was remembered as highly imaginative and able to inspire the same trait in her students; for example, when the classes staged a production of *Joan of Arc*, she purchased dishcloths, dipped them in silver paint, and sewed them together to create "chain mail" for the actors' armor.[10] This ingenuity with limited resources impressed Dreyfuss and informed his development as a stage designer — in which creating the greatest degree of illusion with a minimum of expenditure often meant the difference between success and failure. Miss Mueden became Dreyfuss's lifelong friend.

The earliest known extant artworks by Dreyfuss date from this period. The first is the cover illustration of a program for Class Day at the Ethical Culture school, which featured a performance of *The Man Who Married a Dumb Wife* by Anatole France (the program also served as a dance card). Dreyfuss's illustration is of a woman in late

medieval costume, accompanied by two floral sidebars alongside its single-line frame. It is dated May 19, 1922, and initialed "HD" in the lower right-hand corner. The program was hand-tinted in watercolor and bears a strong resemblance to two later costume studies (c. 1923–28) by Dreyfuss now in the Drawings and Prints Department at the National Design Museum (1973–15–129, –130).

The level of Dreyfuss's creative ability at the end of his formal education is evident in two other drawings now in the museum's collection (1973–15–115, –117). One is the floor plan, dated June 13, 1922, of an "ideal house" with two wings culminating in octagonal towers. While rudimentary in execution, the plan shows some imaginative thinking on Dreyfuss's part, whereby he separated the children's and the servants' quarters from the master bedroom, retaining a large, flexible space in the central living area. The second, undated drawing shows the exterior elevation of the same dwelling. One tower

Class day program for 1922. The earliest extant work from Dreyfuss's hand reveals a decorative quality seldom encountered except in personal notes to friends and family. His monogram appears in the lower right-hand corner.

from this drawing appears in faint pencil outlines on the floor plan, so it was probably done at the same time. The exterior elevation is more crisply rendered than the floor plan and displays an elegant style that is missing from its companion.

The excellent education that Dreyfuss received during his last two years of high school helped set high standards for the future designer. He had learned enough about fine art, crafts, and artistic processes to be comfortable in these realms later in life and to exercise the "inherent good taste" that he felt existed within most people.[11] He had discovered a world of high ideals tempered by practicality in the example set by Elliott, and he had found a calling in stage design from working on pageants and festivals with Miss Mueden. Dreyfuss was well equipped to handle the challenges he would confront in the coming decade.

During the summer following his graduation Dreyfuss was the assistant leader of a group of ten women from the school who toured Europe. This was his first trip abroad. He visited sites and monuments the night before the group did, "cramming" in preparation for guiding their visits. He gained enough experience and confidence to work some six years later as a guide for American Express.

Upon his return, a further scholarship awaited him, again made available through the munificence of the Society for Ethical Culture.[12] This allowed him to study with Norman Bel Geddes, who was then making his mark in the theater and was teaching a course in theatrical design at his own New York studio.[13] While there is a limited amount of material on the relationship between Bel Geddes as teacher and Dreyfuss as student, it is readily apparent that the younger man was infused with Bel Geddes's enthusiasm, air of progressivism in the theatrical arts, and range of ambition. The fact that each had little to say about the other seems to have discouraged examination of this crucial relationship. Ultimately, Bel Geddes's example was probably the determining factor in Dreyfuss's decision to follow him from stage design into the field of industrial design. Dreyfuss refers in his personal records to a "Course with Norman Bel Geddes in Theatrical Design" that ran through the winter of 1922–23, and notes that he remained "to assist him in theatre work for 1½ years after" until 1924 (it seems he actually continued to take classes from Bel Geddes through the spring of 1924).[14] After finishing with the academic part of the class, Dreyfuss stayed on as "one of many assistants to Norman Bel Geddes during the time the settings for 'The Miracle' were made."[15] Along with other student apprentices, Dreyfuss helped create a scale model for a special stage designed to present Dante Alighieri's *Divine Comedy* (including some two hundred miniature costumed figures). The progress of the performance had been mapped out previously through sixty-four drawings, one for every other minute of the production.[16] In a letter

Norman Bel Geddes. Masterful both at inspiring others and anticipating the demands of his visionary stage settings, Bel Geddes was to Dreyfuss the sole genius among the first generation of industrial designers in the United States. Bel Geddes's failure to see some of his most important projects to completion no doubt led Dreyfuss to a more measured approach regarding the changes he hoped to make in society.

to his former teacher, Dreyfuss recalls working with the scale models during a photography session:

> You wanted to thicken the atmosphere to emphasize the third dimension and toward this end had built a smoke machine. By two o'clock in the morning the smoke machine was tired. It was a machine and we were human, so you substituted two of us for it. I must have been fifteen and had never smoked in my life. You told [Mordecai] Gor[e]lick and me to sit under the model and keep three cigarettes going all the time, puffing like mad for ten to fifteen minutes without a breather. While you yelled to Brug[u]iere, — Hold it Francis; wait for the atmosphere. More Henry, more! *I thought to myself, I would only do it for him.* Whenever I look through that nice book of pictures I remember that I was the smoke. [The emphasis is Dreyfuss's; he would have been eighteen on March 2, 1922.][17]

Curiously, Dreyfuss is not among the students listed by Bel Geddes in his 1924 publication *A Project for a Theatrical Presentation of The Divine Comedy of Dante Alighieri.* According to Dreyfuss, it was the stage designer's excessive demands that caused him to quit.[18] It is reasonable to suppose that he left sometime between the photo session and the published results. Bel Geddes had moderately nice things to say about his former pupil; he found him "honest, straight from the shoulder, there's nothing phoney about him, he's square — just a good human being."[19] He made no specific statements about his pupil's strengths or weaknesses as a designer.

Dreyfuss referred to Bel Geddes as "genius #1 in my life" in recalling his early years. When asked by a younger colleague in the industrial design field to evaluate Bel Geddes's contribution, he said, "I believe that Norman Bel Geddes is the only authentic genius this profession has ever produced."[20] From Bel Geddes's perspective Dreyfuss was "apprentice, office boy, and then assistant, for the first three years of my professional life." Dreyfuss summarized Bel Geddes's role in creating the profession: "To be an industrial designer is to breathe an atmosphere that Norman Bel Geddes helped to create."[21] He described his teacher as "a master of stage lighting," a critical aspect of stage design as well as industrial design to Dreyfuss.[22]

It is worth examining what Dreyfuss might have learned from Bel Geddes over the course of three years. For this we have to turn to Bel Geddes's notes for his lectures on stage design.[23] While they tend to lack specificity, these notes are worth consideration in light of Dreyfuss's later practices as a designer:

> Design is mental conception of something to be expressed. It is [an] organism of correlative parts, the relation of part to part and the parts to the whole.
> — Principle of designing building, painting, music, poems, or drama the same.
> — Value of form lies in its ability to express significance clearly.
> — Preliminary visualization . . . Reduce problem to fundamentals . . . Discriminate against unessentials. See problem in terms of voids and solids.

On first reading, these statements seem so broad that they could be applied to almost any artistic pursuit. They point, however, to what would become fundamental truths for the first generation of American industrial designers. In the first statement, the importance of the coordination of the parts of a designed object and their sub-ordination to the whole would provide the rationale for Dreyfuss's "cleanlining" of machines that resulted in stunning "before and after" images that helped sell the profession to the general public.[24] The notion conveyed in Bel Geddes's second statement is that design provides an "umbrella" or a coordinating principle for the disciplines of architecture, product design, fine art, and craft. This is essential to both men's ideas about their broad-based activities, and it is tied to the issue of industrial design's debt to stage design. Regarding form and clarity, a mainstay of the Dreyfuss firm's design activities during its mature phase would be the rationalization of the positions of controls, their legibility, and the ease of operation. The firm's generic designs — for example, the Model 500 telephone, the Honeywell "round" thermostat,

Henry Dreyfuss at age twenty-three, around the time he began designing sets for the Mark Strand Theatre.

and other projects of the postwar period — stood in contrast to a tendency by lesser design teams to rely on automotive and aviation motifs to appeal to the public. In avoiding such derivativeness, Dreyfuss hoped his designs would be outmoded not by stylistic shifts in interior decoration and popular taste but by technological obsolescence. His decisions reflected an attempt to satisfy a range of demands with the technology available at the time of their creation. In their appearance, Dreyfuss stressed the significance of the object as an achievement of its time.

Dreyfuss felt that Bel Geddes was a futurist, in the sense that his ideas were directed several years or even decades ahead.[25] Perhaps seeing so few of Bel Geddes's brilliant ideas reach fruition made Dreyfuss especially aware of the importance of staying in the realm of the achievable when working with manufacturers and other clients. Part of Dreyfuss's contribution to the new profession was demonstrating that the industrial designer need not be an impresario like Bel Geddes in order to achieve substantial results.

Henry Dreyfuss's first independent stage design was for a 1923 production in Detroit of a comedy by Anthony Wharton, *The Heart of Cellini*. Produced at the New Detroit Theatre, it rarely appears in accounts of Dreyfuss's stage career. Lionel Atwill, an actor and director with whom Dreyfuss worked repeatedly during the next twelve years, was cast in the lead, and the play was produced by B. C. Whitney.[26]

During the same period, Dreyfuss courted the management of the Mark Strand Theatre, which found itself caught in the transition from stage productions to motion pictures.[27] Dreyfuss's work with the Mark Strand Theatre dates from the e nd of August 1923.[28] In his record of personal statistics, Dreyfuss summarizes the experience with manager Joseph Plunkett: "Wrote to manager criticizing setting for feature movies, asking for interview. Finally given job at $50 per week; thereafter for 5 years supervised all scenery, costumes, lighting, equipment, etc. As shows changed weekly, designed and produced 52 entire new shows a year — over 250 shows." These shows probably consisted of a number of short vaudeville skits or musical numbers between films. All did not go smoothly during these first years. An early setting for a jazz band, featuring a stylish peacock in black and white, gave Plunkett pause — the bird was considered an ill omen in theatrical circles.[29] Another interviewer had Dreyfuss as an initial success but recalls a similar story about the theater's manager and the bird:

> The boy's first effort was a success; dressing the ballet in oilcloth, he caused it to impersonate a museum of porcelain statues. He made gorgeous sketches for a peacock ballet; Plunkett was astonished that so smart a boy didn't know that a peacock was the worst bad luck that can befall a theater. Dreyfuss quickly demoted the birds to turkeys.[30]

Dreyfuss himself recalled an episode when enthusiasm for his own ideas got the best of him:

> At the Strand in New York, I worked out an atmospheric bit for an act called Gerry and Her Baby Grands, a four-piano team. Instead of having the four instruments placed all over the stage, I dreamed up the idea of a huge simulated piano encompassing the width of all four keyboards. It was finished just in time for the opening performance, at which point I discovered it was too big to move through the stage entrance.[31]

Unfortunately, no photographs of stage designs for the Strand can be attributed to Dreyfuss with certainty. He enjoyed a good relationship with Joseph Plunkett, whom he used as a reference in his application for membership in the United Scenic Artists' Association. The discipline required to produce some 250 shows over the course of five years must have tempered Dreyfuss's upstart qualities (he continually referred to himself as "brash" in recalling his twenties).[32]

In 1925 Dreyfuss was working on the stage settings for *Deep in the Woods* at the Auditorium Theatre in Baltimore.[33] Lionel Atwill both directed and played the male lead. The following year, Dreyfuss leaped to Broadway with the sets for *Beau Gallant*, which debuted at the Ritz Theatre on April 5, again with Atwill

Dreyfuss's flamboyant signature is found on a number of his surviving drawings for stage designs. Later it appeared on his famous Thermos carafe and the Birtman Visible Toaster (shown on page 112).

as the principal actor. Dreyfuss then endured an eighteen-month hiatus between Broadway shows. During that time, in addition to the weekly revues for the Strand Theatre, he worked on "traveling vaudeville units" for the Keith-Albee theater consortium and designed costumes for *The Merry Wives of Windsor*. The costume studies for this production are in the Drawings and Prints Department at the National Design Museum. Dated 1927, they are executed in watercolor and show a firmness of outline, saturation of color, and freeness of movement in the figures depicted. They are among the best work from Dreyfuss's own hand.

Within four years of starting his professional career, Dreyfuss's fees for his services increased markedly. John Zanft of the Fox Theatre Circuit offered him the position of art director and raised his weekly salary to $250 at the end of 1927.[34] In the letter, Zanft stated that "any time you are assigned to perform services in any theatre out of New York City, this corporation will pay your railroad fares and allow you $7.50 per day to cover every other form of expense." Trips to Philadelphia were commonplace.

In spite of the considerable leap in pay from his salary at the Strand Theatre, Dreyfuss was apparently not content with this position; he worked for the Fox Theatre Circuit for less than three months in 1928. Louis Brecker, a friend and the owner of the Roseland Ballrooms in Manhattan and Brooklyn, recalled this period in a letter he wrote years later to Dreyfuss's secretary Rita Hart:

> I recall he worked for Fox...and had charge of the stage sets in Philadelphia but he could not stand his bosses — so one day he told them off and quit the job. He then went to Europe not knowing what he was going to do but went just to forget everything.[35]

Dreyfuss's short period of employment with the Fox organization is confirmed by a letter written in Tunis on March 17, 1928:

> I have enjoyed my vacation immensely so far and believe the rest has done me a great deal of good. What I am going to do upon my return, I don't know as yet — I've had several offers of positions but haven't definitely decided.[36]

A newspaper interviewer recounted this same period:

> He went to Paris. Then to North Africa. When his savings petered out, he took a job as guide for American Express. Having accumulated enough money to go home, he returned by way of Paris, where he found a huge stack of accumulated mail. Before he could get it read, a Paris representative of R. H. Macy called to ask, with some annoyance, "Don't you ever read letters?"[37]

These anecdotes reveal a versatile young man who was not afraid to "wing it" over unfamiliar territory. Dreyfuss does not disclose what was going through his mind during this period. Had he really gone abroad after precipitously quitting a well-paying job "just to forget everything" as Brecker wrote, or was he mulling over "several offers of positions" (and who might these have been from)? Any comment here is speculation, but perhaps Dreyfuss was trying to figure it all out; perhaps this is the juncture at which he decided to pursue industrial design. Dreyfuss's autobiography, his personal records, and the records of others all give the same account of the next step in his life: upon returning to Paris he is tracked down by the management of Macy's and throws over his "vacation plans" to return to New York. He had been promised a chance to evaluate their merchandise for redesign. One author characterized the episode as follows:

Oswald Knauth, an executive of Macy's ... told him to wander around the 100-odd departments and redesign anything he didn't like ... on being asked to inspect and criticize, he [Dreyfuss] was shocked by everything he saw. He examined hundreds of objects from pocket knives to electric stoves and disliked every one.... Although he was flat broke, Dreyfuss turned down the department-store job. He had promised himself that he would be his own boss.... He felt also that the big idea had one important defect: it overlooked the fact that a manufacturer could seldom change the design of a product without scrapping valuable machinery and retooling his plant at great expense. It was useless, according to Dreyfuss, for a retailer to bombard manufacturers with random suggestions.[38]

This illuminating story readily separates Dreyfuss from other early industrial designers. Not only on this occasion, but on many others, Dreyfuss refused to accept the conditions imposed by a client. He refused to compromise at the start of a project when he did not feel the parameters set provided for a true rethinking of a product's design beginning with the manufacturing process itself. Unless he could consult directly with the people who would be responsible for making, as well as marketing, a product, his design innovations might be compromised or even made impossible by the conditions prevailing at the place of manufacture. In discussing the theoretical component of Dreyfuss's approach to design, it becomes clear that a round-table approach, involving all parties concerned, became one of his most important contributions to an industrial designer's job.

Dreyfuss's friend Louis Brecker may have given him the best advice he had received about his career up to this point:

While on the way back [from Europe] he received an offer from Macy's to design their modern silverware, etc. as a permanent job. I urged him not to take it but to go out for himself. I even sent him around to some of my friends to get him started — and you know what has happened since.[39]

Unfortunately, the names of Brecker's referrals remain unidentified. Dreyfuss's transition from stage designer to industrial designer was neither quick nor easy. In fact, his career as an industrial designer and as a stage designer overlapped by six years, although one would never receive this impression from his autobiography. Up to 1930, he had executed stage designs for only a handful of major shows that made it to opening night. During this same period he received modest assignments, redesigning such products as children's furniture, glass containers, and temporary exhibitions. Ironically, he had been referring to himself as an industrial designer for two years when he experienced his greatest successes as a stage designer.

"Two-headed industrial designer at the client's roundtable," c. 1955. Dreyfuss emphasized, in his many written accounts of his practice from the early 1930s, the critical importance of meeting with all departments concerned with the production and marketing of new designs.

In 1930 Dreyfuss's career began a remarkable advance on both the industrial and the stage design fronts. His output as a stage designer was prodigious: sets for nine separate shows were completed in 1930 and four more in 1931. Bill Purcell, Dreyfuss's right-hand man in the South Pasadena, California, office during its existence, recalled reading that Dreyfuss had five shows running on Broadway at one time in 1930.[40] When his designs were mentioned in reviews, the attitude of the critics was generally favorable and showed an appreciation of his technical skills. A high point was reached in *The Last Mile*, by John Wexley, a production of 1930 that starred Spencer Tracy. Dreyfuss's design of a line of death-row jail cells was admired for "a cell-block that clangs when the steel doors are thrown open," and his approach to stage design was considered very practical and well-researched by the standards of the day.[41] In search of a "morbidly accurate" setting, Dreyfuss went so far as to contact twenty-five prison wardens in order to discover if there was any "standard type" of death-row architecture. (In the process, he discovered that there was no typical death row and that there was no capital punishment in Kansas, the location in which the fictional account was initially set.)[42]

Dreyfuss's sets often garnered more acclaim than did the plays. Of *Sweet Stranger*, a play from 1930, a critic stated that "what keeps it from being entirely just another of those Broadway things are Henry Dreyfuss's Tiffany backgrounds."[43] Among Dreyfuss's most often cited and visually interesting efforts were the sets for *The Cat and the Fiddle* by Jerome Kern, where "Brussels is quite satisfactory for artistic romance and it gives Henry Dreyfuss an opportunity to sketch sidewalk cafés and somberly colored quays and lavish apartments and two traditional scenes on a theatre stage."[44] Photographs of the sets now in the Dreyfuss Collection demonstrate that he was capable of illusionistic turns in the design of a scrim curtain as well as expressionist effects in his townscape for the same production.[45]

Dreyfuss's last design for the stage, the settings for Humphrey Cobb's *Paths of Glory*, provoked one critic to write, "meeting the scenic requirements of 'Paths of Glory' called for ingenuity, inspiration and a superior sense of the practical." For this production Dreyfuss designed the settings "in thirteen scenes, which moved on three rolling platforms from scene to scene without delay." Scenes changed "rapidly from place to place in the war zone, and we are shown realistic reproductions of company headquarters, a café behind the lines, front-line dugouts, observation posts, and finally a deserted château, where the court-martial scene takes place."[46] Other critics admired Dreyfuss's use of space, his angled perspective, and economy of settings. One critic viewed the settings as a series of "realistic reproductions," while another saw them as "semi-impressionistic, pitched against swathing curtains of gray."[47]

On one occasion, Henry Dreyfuss acted as director as well as stage designer for a production. For *Continental Varieties* of 1934, a showcase for European talent, Dreyfuss

Stage set for *The Last Mile*, 1930. The year 1930 marked a break-through
for Dreyfuss as a stage designer. His sets for *The Last Mile*, which starred
Spencer Tracy, were praised for their gritty details. A thorough investigation of
real death rows lay behind his grimly realistic environments. A scale model
shows that Dreyfuss paid special attention to the lighting of the set; he was
familiar with the state of the art from his association with Bel Geddes and
Eddie Kook of Century Lighting.

SCENE I

-THE GANG'S ALL HERE-
PRODUCTION OF GREEN, GENSLER CORP.

SCALE
ACT

DRAWING NO.
PLATE NO.
DATE

THIS DRAWING IS MY PERSONAL PROPERTY
AND MUST BE RETURNED TO ME

DREYFUSS 580 FIFTH AVENUE · NEW YORK

Above: RKO Orpheum Theatre, Denver, Colorado, main floor, 1931. Dreyfuss's borrowings from European sources were tempered, but clearly the influence of French art moderne was upon him in creating the decorative scheme for this major space.

Top left: Backdrop for *The Gang's All Here*, 1931. One of the most colorful and animated of Dreyfuss's surviving works, this circus tent with its menagerie of cartoon-like creatures may have suggested the motif for the children's nursery of the RKO Orpheum Theatre of the same year.

Bottom left: Set design for *The Gang's All Here*, 1931. An up-to-the-minute stylishness pervaded the sets for this musical starring Ted Healey and Ruby Keeler. It is easy to see in this context how Dreyfuss made the leap from set design to the interior design of theaters.

RKO Orpheum Theatre, Davenport, Iowa, basement lounge, 1931.
A hodge-podge of influences tempered by Dreyfuss's own personality are seen
here. The furnishings and carpet have a distinctly Viennese quality, while
the plaster bas-relief panel initially strikes one as French-inspired. The subject,
the filming of a Hollywood movie, is unmistakably American and appropriate.
Dreyfuss lit the venetian blinds from behind to dispel any lingering gloominess
in this basement lounge.

redecorated the theater, wrapped the seats in white, and placed full-length caricatures of the leading theatrical critics of the day in the lounge. He whipped the performance into shape in a mere four days and eight hours. Not the least of his problems was communicating with the international cast, and he was forced to rely on pantomime to put across his points about their performances (even mimicking a number of dances to indicate to Vicente Escudero the order in which he wanted them performed). Dreyfuss managed to be a hit with both management and performers.[48]

Success on Broadway brought Dreyfuss considerable public attention at the time he was making the transition to industrial design. His reputation for pragmatic problem-solving and his longstanding relationships with theatrical clients were strong recommendations in his favor when he approached businessmen. He was a tough negotiator; involved in a number of disputes with United Scenic Artists of America, he was active in defining the role of the industrial designer versus the stage designer. A primary concern was the very overlap in the fields he had been exploiting. He struggled to make it clear to the president of United Scenic Artists that in working as an interior designer for Radio-Keith-Orpheum Theaters he was not in conflict with the working rules or the constitution of the union. Dreyfuss won the argument in 1931.[49]

Dreyfuss had begun as a consultant for RKO in connection with a new movie theater the organization had built in Sioux City, Iowa. He was a keen observer of human nature, and the story about this early project became one of the favorites told in the ensuing years:

Dreyfuss, then a young theatrical scene designer, was sent to Sioux City, Iowa, by his employers, the Radio-Keith-Orpheum circuit, to find out why a brand-new, beautifully decorated movie palace in that metropolis was drawing nothing but large quantities of Iowa atmosphere. After Dreyfuss arrived, he lowered the prices, ran triple features and gave away enough dishes to equip a cafeteria—but still the majority of the populace wandered past his theater and into an unventilated flea-bag movie house down the street. Finally, Dreyfuss decided to make a scientific study of the matter.

For three days he stood outside his theater and watched the reactions of the people walking by. Then he ordered his staff to remove the expensive, deep-pile scarlet carpet from the lobby, and replace it with a plain rubber mat. Almost miraculously, and from that time forth, the RKO theater was jammed.

Dreyfuss simply had discovered that the farmers and the townsfolk had been ashamed of messing up that gorgeous carpet with their muddy boots and galoshes.[50]

The RKO theaters in Davenport, Iowa, and Denver, Colorado, were Dreyfuss's next major projects. He attempted no radical innovations in these two theaters but aimed for a greater sense of unity in their interiors than was evident in many of their Art Deco counterparts. He dictated the following passage close to the time of the completion of the Davenport Orpheum:

This is the first theatre in which a designer has been called in to correlate every detail. Usually the architect does the plaster work, the carpet man the carpet, the seat man the seat covers, etcetera. On this occasion Mr. Plunkett was kind enough to call this organization in and let us do the entire job so that the result would be harmonious. In other words the carpet was designed thinking of the walls, the walls were designed thinking of the ceiling, the fixtures were designed thinking of the seat-ends, etcetera. From the base[ment] lounge to the last seat in the balcony there is one thought in design. No two schools have ever been used. Everything is in direct harmony.[51]

The Dreyfuss theater was characterized by a tempered approach to Art Deco motifs, predominantly simple geometric and stylized floral patterns with an emphasis on visually sumptuous materials, moiré wallpapers, pierced plaster grillwork, and leather armchairs. The men's lounge displayed silver wallcoverings manufactured by Salubra AG, wood molding and wainscoting of black ebony, flat black carpeting, and leather uphol-

Photomontage of Dreyfuss's first office for industrial design at 218 West 48th Street in New York, established in 1928. Two years later, his move to 580 Fifth Avenue signaled that he intended to leave the theater and the theater district behind; it took him five more years to realize the former.

stery in brilliant vermilion. Theatrical lighting effects appeared in the ladies' lounge, where vanities were lit from below (perhaps more impressive atmospherically than helpful in applying makeup). Concealed lighting illuminated false windows in the basement placed behind venetian blinds. The only "fine art" commissioned for the project was a low-relief plaster sculpture depicting a thoroughly modern scene: the shooting of a Hollywood movie. Dreyfuss even displayed a whimsical side: a children's playroom was given a circus tent theme.[52]

Architecturally, innovations were tempered as well: Dreyfuss noted that "the absence of any definite proscenium arch (or really the enlargement of the proscenium arch to take in a good part of the theater), helps make this theater a bit more intimate than the average. There is no definite frame dividing the audience from the stage."[53] The overall conception was of luxury without ostentation, with facilities and furniture that were meant to make people comfortable. This conception of interior design held true for Dreyfuss's interiors for both the New York Central Railroad's 20th Century Limited train and the American Export Line's S.S. *Constitution* and S.S. *Independence*, created during the 1930s and 1950s, respectively.

Dreyfuss cited 1928 in his record of personal statistics as the year in which he opened an office "for theatrical work, and [the] start of industrial design activities." Two years passed before he achieved anything of note in the latter. When Dreyfuss contacted Emma Mueden at the Society for Ethical Culture's school, stating that he was looking for additional help with his business, she sent him Doris Marks. Dreyfuss was looking

Doris Marks was cited as one of 10 Most Important Women of the Year by the *Los Angeles Times* in 1963, partly for her work as board member of the Los Angeles County Zoo. The pin she wears was made after a design for the Persian Room.

out of the window in his third-floor office at 218 West 48th Street on that day. A Pierce-Arrow limousine came to a halt on the street below and the chauffeur opened the door for a young woman carrying an umbrella with a bulldog handle. After cautioning the driver not to wait in front of the building, she disappeared into its entrance. She then appeared in Dreyfuss's office for an interview, unaware that he had seen her arrival at the building. They must have made a profound impression upon each other. When Dreyfuss's secretary asked who the woman was after her departure, he replied, "That's the girl I'm going to marry." The next day Doris's father, Marcus Marks, took Dreyfuss to lunch, and when his wife inquired that evening where he had eaten earlier that day, he said, "I had lunch with the boy Doris is going to marry."[54]

Doris Marks was just shy of thirty-one, being one year older than Henry Dreyfuss. She had also attended the Society for Ethical Culture's school on Central Park West in Manhattan and graduated in 1918. It appears that she and her future husband were not

acquainted with each other as students. Following graduation she entered Vassar and majored in psychology.

During the years 1922 to 1927 she traveled extensively in Europe, especially in Italy, where she moved in fashionable circles. Gail Dreyfuss Wilson believed that her mother had been doing social work at the time she met Dreyfuss. Rita Hart, who would work closely with them after 1930, recalled the same.[55]

As the daughter of the former borough president of Manhattan, Doris Marks had numerous contacts within the business and social circles of Manhattan. Her family was wealthy and distinguished. Marcus M. Marks (1858–1934) was noted as "a very good friend" of Andrew Carnegie.[56] As the presi-

Capstan Glass Co., cookie jar, 1932. Dreyfuss, again mining a circus theme, sketched this cookie jar in the shape of an elephant. The detailed clay model suggests that it may have made it to production.

dent of the National Association of Clothiers Marks was able to bring harmony to the affairs of his own line of business and eventually to the woolen, trimming, cloak, fur, and paint trades as well. He worked as a peacemaker in many industrial disputes involving taxi drivers, expressmen, textile workers, hatmakers, boilermakers, conductors, and trainmen. Leaving the daily affairs of his business in charge of his assistants in 1913, he devoted himself full time to politics and social issues. In the same year, he was elected borough president of Manhattan. In this position, during the administration of Mayor John Purroy Mitchel, Marks established a system of open public markets, introduced welfare work among his 2,000 employees, and arranged for joint trial boards for civil service employees.

Interestingly, it was his wife's discovery of the idea of Daylight Saving Time in a German newspaper that provided the starting point for a four-year campaign for the scheme's adoption in the United States (the idea had first been promoted in Germany).[57] Mrs.

Marks was the former Esther Friedman (1867–1937). She and her husband helped found the Tuberculosis Preventorium for Children to combat what was then known as the "white plague." Active in the women's suffrage and birth-control movements, she pressed for the investigation of women's working conditions in the manufacturing and hotel trades through the National Civic Federation. At one time she had been the New York chairwoman of the National Woman's party.[58] The Marks family was living at 4 East 94th Street in 1912, and probably earlier; Doris Marks grew up, not only among wealth, but in an atmosphere permeated by social concerns and high standards.

Dreyfuss's early industrial design projects (1929–1930) were minor and tentative, but in 1930, Dreyfuss moved his office to 580 Fifth Avenue, a signal that Dreyfuss had decided that the time had come to push ahead with industrial design and leave theater design (it would take another five years before this transpired). This new office was outside of the theater district, with Doris Marks as executive business head. His staff consisted of Rita Hart as secretary and bookkeeper (later office manager), and Herbert Barnhart and Julian G. Everett as designers. Miss Marks and Miss Hart (as they were always known in the office) were referred to as partners by Henry Dreyfuss in his own records. Henry's brother, Arnold, was also working for the office at this time, but did not stay with the business long; he married and moved to La Cañada, California, where he died at age thirty (his health had been poor since childhood).

Gruen Watch Makers Guild, packaging for Carré watch, 1930. Whether Dreyfuss was repackaging an existing Gruen design or was the author of the total concept is uncertain; he claimed this as one of his first industrial designs. The packaging for this woman's purse or pocket watch followed up on the notion of the watch's unique case, which, when open, acted to support it as a travel clock.

Rita Hart is the person most knowledgeable about the working relationship that existed between Dreyfuss and Doris Marks. She says that he had an excellent business sense, which was complemented by his wife's organizational skills. While he was the "creative genius" of the two, she exercised considerable influence over the flow of work in the office and its personnel selections. She sought to move Dreyfuss out of the realm of the theater and into industrial design, and discouraged him from his natural inclination to accommodate the large numbers of people interested in his services.[59] She insisted that he charge substantial fees for his work, feeling that anything less would prove detrimental to the status of the fledgling profession.[60]

Henry Dreyfuss and Doris Marks were married on July 26, 1930, in a civil ceremony at the Municipal Building in New York. Their honeymoon was spent on a train (where they went is not noted). They took up residence in the Tuscany at 120 East 39th Street, where they wrote to Emma Mueden about their mutual happiness. He thanked her for being his "Guardian Angel" who "always more or less looked over me and steered me around."[61]

It is clear that Doris Marks was important to the success of the firm. Analyzing her impact on the formal elements of their designs, however, remains a difficult task. Both husband and wife disavowed any contribution by her to the way things looked. In interviews with their contemporaries, the impression of her personal taste that emerged ranged from refined to very particular. One young woman in the office was delegated the task of returning items that Dreyfuss bought for his wife on trips — usually on the basis that they were extravagances. Doris Marks probably reinforced Dreyfuss's appreciation of simplicity and things European. The aesthetic of the Henry Dreyfuss firm would be influential for what it did not, in fact, include: the pandering to popular taste that characterized much of the coming "design decade's" production.

Notes

1. The facts about Dreyfuss's formative years can be verified, to some extent, through documents other than his own recollections. Dreyfuss, "A Record of Personal and Business Vital Statistics," unpaginated oversize file, Dreyfuss Collection, Industrial Design Archives, Cooper-Hewitt, National Design Museum, Smithsonian Institution (hereafter referred to as Dreyfuss Collection), 1972-88.178. Dreyfuss's letter to his son, John, October 4, 1972.

2. Beverly Smith, "He's into Everything," *American Magazine* 113 (April 1932), 43.

3. Horace J. Bridges, s.v. "Ethical Culture Movement," *1939 Britannica Book of the Year* (Chicago: Encyclopedia Britannica, 1939).

4. Jeffrey L. Meikle was the first scholar to point out the impact of these lessons on Dreyfuss's life. See *Twentieth Century Limited: Industrial Design in the United States, 1925–1939* (Philadelphia: Temple University Press, 1979), 57.

5. *Ethical Culture School: Prevocational Art Department* (New York: John C. Powers Co., 1921), 11–27.

6. Ibid.

7. Dreyfuss, "The little I know about my family background," letter to his son, 1972.

8. Elliott had a distinguished career as both an educator and a progressive social activist. He founded the Hudson Guild Neighborhood House in Manhattan's Chelsea neighborhood in 1895 with his own resources, seeking to provide children with recreational activities other than the gang warfare that was rife along the waterfront. In 1938 he founded the Central Good Neighbor Committee, which attempted to put democracy and racial tolerance on a firmer footing, and aided refugees coming to the United States. In addition, he organized the School for Printers' Apprentices, was president of the National Federation of Settlements, and in 1926 was the head of the United Neighborhood Houses of New York.

9. Information on Elliott comes from "Dr. John L. Elliott is Dead Here at 73," *New York Times*, April 13, 1942; "The Late John Lovejoy Elliott," *New York Times*, April 14, 1942 (which corrects errors made in the previous article); "Dr. John Elliott Dead; Hudson Guild Founder," *New York Herald Tribune*, April 13, 1942; and Nannette Rothschild, interviewed by Frieda Moss, transcript of tape recording made in 1963. All materials courtesy Ethical Culture/Fieldston School Archives, New York.

10. This anecdote and other information on Emma Mueden were related to the author in a telephone conversation with Barbara Michaels of the Ethical Culture/Fieldston School Archives in May 1991.

11. "All for Joe and Josephine," *Architectural Record* 118 (July 1955), 48. The phrase is originally found in Dreyfuss, *Designing for People* (New York: Simon and Schuster, 1955), 97: "Most people have inherent good taste, but they can't be expected to use it if they can't find good things." Swiss designer Max Bill felt differently: "The persistent cultivation of this myth (of public taste) is the unhappy hunting ground of unscrupulous manufacturers and middlemen who employ all the resources of publicity to persuade the consumer (which in such cases means everybody) that the myth is reality." *Form: A Balance Sheet of Mid-Twentieth Century Trends in Design* (Basel, 1952), quoted in Terence Riley and Edward Eigen, "Between the Museum and the Marketplace: Selling Good Design," *Studies in Modern Art* 4 (1994), 170.

12. Carlton Atherton, "Henry Dreyfuss: Designer," *Design* 36 (January 1935), 5.

13. Bel Geddes probably taught the stage design course as a source of income and unpaid assistants. It was offered from 1921 through 1927. Norman Bel Geddes to Mrs. George F. Dalton, November 19, 1928, Design Course/SC-3/j.-4, Norman Bel Geddes Collection, Hoblitzelle Theatre Arts Library, Henry Ransom Humanities Research Center, University of Texas at Austin (hereafter referred to as Bel Geddes Collection). This and other information on Dreyfuss's studies with Bel Geddes were provided by Jeffrey L. Meikle.

14. Dreyfuss, "A Record of Personal and Business Vital Statistics." "Incidentally, I want to explain why I have been to so few meetings [of the United Scenic Artists' Association]. Last summer I signed an application to take a course each Friday night — for twenty weeks. I have been attending these lectures and they have interfered with my coming to your meetings." Dreyfuss to Carl Lessing, March 29, 1924, United Scenic Artists Local 829 Archives, New York. Lessing was president of United Scenic Artists in New York. The author's assumption that these are classes with Bel Geddes is based on the fact that Dreyfuss refers to no other such classes anywhere in his personal records or interviews.

15. Gilbert Seldes, "Profiles: Artist in a Factory," *The New Yorker* 7 (August 29, 1931), 22. For additional information on *The Miracle*, see Oliver Martin Sayler, ed., *The Miracle* (souvenir program) (New York: Theatre International, 1924). The full title of the latter is "F. Ray Comstock and Morris Gest present for the first time in America the stupendous, spectacular pantomime The Miracle, staged by Max Reinhardt, book by Karl Vollmoeller, score by Engelbert Humperdinck, revised and extended by Friedrich Schirmer, production designed by Norman Bel Geddes, built by P. J. Carey & Co., entire production under the supervision of Morris Gest." Bel Geddes's stage

set for the Century Theatre was featured for its innovations in Albert A. Hopkins, "A Theatre Without a Stage," *Scientific American* 130 (April 1924), 228–29.

16. Norman Bel Geddes, *A Project for a Theatrical Presentation of The Divine Comedy of Dante Alighieri* (New York: Theatre Arts, 1924).

17. Bel Geddes, manuscript for autobiography, Jamaica version, chapters 48–52, Bel Geddes Collection.

18. Kimmis Hendrick, "Questions Trigger the Flash," *Christian Science Monitor*, May 11–13, 1968 (weekend issue), sec. 2, p. 1.

19. Bel Geddes, manuscript for autobiography, Jamaica version, chapter 76: transcript of interview with Bel Geddes by Selma Robinson of *PM*, January 27, 1942, Bel Geddes Collection.

20. Dreyfuss, "The little I know about my family background." Arnold Wolf, cited by Edward Zagorski, "Design Heads & Tales: An Anecdotal History of Industrial Design," *Innovation* (Journal of the Industrial Designers Society of America) 10 (Spring 1991), 33.

21. Dreyfuss, in "Norman Bel Geddes (1893–1958)," *Industrial Design* 5 (June 1958), 51.

22. "Incidentally, he [Dreyfuss] couldn't stand bad lighting, for instance. He would complain about lighting along the top of a bookshelf that had some dark spots between the lamps — that wouldn't worry me, but Henry couldn't stand it. His lighting . . . had to be absolutely even, and that was the stage work of the early years. He was a perfectionist at that sort of thing." William F. H. Purcell, interview with author, March 16–17, 1991. Dreyfuss also became fast friends early in his career with Edward F. Kook, later president of Century Lighting Company in New York.

23. Bel Geddes, "The Objective," lesson 2 of 20 from the elementary level stage design course, Design Course/SC-4/k.-1, Bel Geddes Collection.

24. "The form must be simple and pleasing. I have no sympathy with the thought of applying streamlined shapes to a household utility, but I do believe it can be 'cleanlined' in its design. We have a distinct problem in doing a vacuum cleaner [the Hoover 150]. The outward appearance must impress the consumer with the ease of operation and the design must silently express the many conveniences within the housing." Dreyfuss, "An Industrial Designer Thinks About His Job," in *Art Directors' 18th Annual of Advertising Art* (New York: Longmans Green, 1939), 170.

25. John Dreyfuss, interview with author, November 23, 1990.

26. "Plays and Photoplays: A True Picture of Benvenuto," *Detroit News*, October 16, 1923, *The Heart of Cellini* clippings file, Billy Rose Theatre Collection, Performing Arts Research Center, New York Public Library at Lincoln Center, Astor, Lenox and Tilden Foundations (hereafter referred to as Billy Rose Theatre Collection). The review notes that "'The Heart of Cellini' is Good Atmosphere, But Not Impressive Drama." A program for the performance states that "All settings and costumes in this production designed by Henry Dreyfuss and executed under his direction." *The Heart of Cellini* program file, Billy Rose Theatre Collection.

27. Dreyfuss would tell slightly different versions of the story to interviewers over the years, each emphasizing the upstart quality of his contact with Joseph Plunkett; most cite a letter written by Dreyfuss to Plunkett that verged on insulting the state of the theater's shows, and receiving

a job shortly thereafter, but another version reveals that this was not the case. "At the Strand one night, impressed by the poor settings used for the weekly program, he was provoked into writing a letter to the manager commenting on the inadequate settings used by this popular theatre. The manager asked for suggestions and Mr. Dreyfuss made sketches and went to see him. After two months of sitting on the doorstep for a chance to accost the manager, he obtained an interview and got the job." Atherton, "Henry Dreyfuss: Designer," 6.

28. Dreyfuss to J. F. Plunkett, New York, August 20, 1923, Dreyfuss Collection, 1973-15.23.

29. Seldes, "Profiles: Artist in a Factory," 22.

30. Alva Johnston, "Nothing Looks Right to Dreyfuss," *Saturday Evening Post* (November 22, 1947), 21.

31. Dreyfuss, *Designing for People*, 10.

32. He also used B. C. Whitney, then at the New Amsterdam Theatre, and Norman Bel Geddes as references. He was proposed for membership by an even more distinguished list that included Lee Simonson and Robert Edmond Jones in addition to Bel Geddes. Dreyfuss was elected on January 18 and obligated on February 1, 1924 (not in 1922 as he notes in his record of personal statistics). Henry Dreyfuss file, United Scenic Artists Local 829 Archives, New York. The *New York Times* published an even higher number of productions and a longer term of employment of 416 settings and eight years, respectively, in the announcement of his wedding to Doris Marks in 1930. "Miss Doris Marks Wed to Henry Dreyfuss," *New York Times*, July 30, 1930, 15.

33. From a program for the week of November 9, 1925: "The scenery and costumes designed and constructed under the direction of Henry Dreyfus[s]." *Deep in the Woods* program file, Billy Rose Theatre Collection.

34. John Zanft, vice president and general manager, William Fox Circuit of Theatres, New York, to Dreyfuss, December 31, 1927, Dreyfuss Collection, 1973-15.37.

35. Louis Brecker, New York, to Rita Hart, November 12, 1952, ibid., 1973-15.5.

36. Dreyfuss, Tunis, to Carl Lessing, New York, March 17, 1928, Henry Dreyfuss file, United Scenic Artists Local 829 Archives, New York.

37. Hendrick, "Questions Trigger the Flash," 15. In another version of this story, Dreyfuss revealed that he had been stuck in Tunis after losing all of his money playing roulette during his first night in town. Johnston, "Nothing Looks Right to Dreyfuss," 20–21.

38. Johnston, "Nothing Looks Right to Dreyfuss," 20–21.

39. Brecker to Hart, Dreyfuss Collection, 1973-15.5.

40. William F. H. Purcell, interview with author, March 16–17, 1991.

41. Brooks Atkinson, "The Play: The Last Mile," *New York Times*, February 14, 1930, 21.

42. "Two in the Spotlight," ibid., May 11, 1930, section 9, 2.

43. Atkinson, "The Play: Sweet Stranger," ibid., October 22, 1930.

44. Atkinson, "The Play: Love to a Kern Score," ibid., October 16, 1931, 26.

45. The cell-block scene from *The Last Mile* and the townscape from *The Cat and the Fiddle* are both illustrated in the first edition of Dreyfuss, *Designing for People*, 49.

46. "'Paths of Glory' Seen in New Haven," *New York Times*, September 19, 1935, 29.

47. John Anderson, "Paths of Glory," *New York Evening Journal*, September 27, 1935; Wilellea Waldorf, "War Plays Reach Local Stages as All Europe Arms," *New York Post*, September 20, 1935; "Impressive War Play," *London Daily Telegraph*, September 28, 1935; "Paths of Glory, New Haven," *Variety*, September 18, 1935; all references from *Paths of Glory* scrapbook file, Billy Rose Theatre Collection.

48. Brooks Atkinson, "The Play: Lucienne Boyer, Vicente Escudero and Others in the 'Continental Varieties,'" *New York Times*, October 4, 1934, 18; "Too Many Tongues for Him," *New York World-Telegram*, October 6, 1934, Henry Dreyfuss clippings file, Billy Rose Theatre Collection.

49. See correspondence between Dreyfuss and United Scenic Artists president W. Percival in 1931, Henry Dreyfuss file, United Scenic Artists Local 829 Archives, New York.

50. Bill Davidson, "You Buy Their Dreams," *Collier's* 120 (August 2, 1947), 23; Dreyfuss's less-embellished version of the story appears in Dreyfuss, *Designing for People*, 159.

51. Glued to the back of a photograph of the interior, this typewritten description and others are notes as "Dictated by Henry Dreyfuss 11/14/31"; Dreyfuss Collection, 1973-15.32.

52. Dreyfuss had executed a design for a backdrop with a circus theme for the first act of *The Gang's All Here*, a musical produced in 1931, Cooper-Hewitt, National Design Museum, Drawings and Prints Department, 1973-15.132.

53. Ibid. In 1983 the Davenport Orpheum was rechristened the Adler after undergoing extensive restoration and renovation. Its appearance is substantially the same as when it first opened.

54. Dreyfuss, "The little I know about my family background."

55. Gail Dreyfuss Wilson, interview with author, November 23, 1990; Rita Hart, interview with author, February 5, 1991.

56. Apparently Marks and Carnegie were golfing partners. It is a coincidence that the Doris and Henry Dreyfuss Memorial Study Center is located in the former Andrew Carnegie mansion, now the Cooper-Hewitt, National Design Museum.

57. "Marcus M. Marks Dies in Hospital," *New York Times*, August 27, 1934, 15. Other information comes from scrapbooks held by Doris and Henry Dreyfuss's children.

58. "Mrs. Marcus Marks, a Welfare Leader," ibid., April 24, 1937, 23.

59. Gail Dreyfuss Wilson, interview with author, November 23, 1990; William F. H. Purcell, interview with author, March 16–17, 1991. Some of Dreyfuss's difficulties in getting paid for his theatrical work are documented in the Henry Dreyfuss file, United Scenic Artists Local 829 Archives, New York.

60. Rita Hart, interview with author, February 5, 1991.

61. "Miss Doris Marks Wed to Henry Dreyfuss," 15; letter from Henry Dreyfuss and Doris Marks Dreyfuss to Emma Mueden, August 19, 1930; it was returned to the Dreyfusses by Miss Mueden on one of their subsequent wedding anniversaries. A photocopy was provided by Gail Dreyfuss Wilson.

Hoover Co., Model 305 vacuum cleaner, 1940. As in the tractor and locomotive designs at the end of the 1930s, the pure teardrop forms of streamlining had given way to a more complex form seen in this vacuum cleaner.

Chapter 2: THE 1930S

HENRY DREYFUSS BECOMES AN

INDUSTRIAL DESIGNER

IN HIS *DESIGNING FOR PEOPLE* of 1955, part autobiography, part "how-to" book, Henry Dreyfuss presents a carefully controlled account of his personal history and development as a designer. The book gives the reader a sense of his accomplishments and his temperament. His stance can be described as obliging, presuming his audience to have little knowledge of industrial design and little interest in his personal life. He tempers his sometimes dry accounts of the design process with an anecdote at the end of each chapter. Some of these provide a chuckle, and others seem a bit strained, as if such admissions as encountering problems or even mild embarrassments were not in character for him. In fact, Henry Dreyfuss was a masterful storyteller to his friends and a riveting performer in front of clients. If his book is a little dull, it is because he deliberately made it that way. He left out the personal impact the world of design had on him — a world of deadlines, budgets, critics, and managers — in which he had to depend on others to realize his ideas. There was a time, as well, when there were no others, when Dreyfuss had struck out on his own from theatrical design, renting a second-floor office at 218 West 48th Street in Manhattan, and furnishing it with a borrowed card table, two folding chairs, a telephone, and a twenty-five-cent philodendron plant. There he confronted a reality that had no doubt struck his elders Norman Bel Geddes and Walter Dorwin Teague only a year or two earlier: billing yourself as an industrial designer was not enough to make the world beat a path to your door. Jobs would have to be solicited. This chapter is an examination of how Dreyfuss made his start in industrial design, and the seminal events that propelled him from the status of novice to major practitioner in the new field within a decade.

While there is no written documentation giving us the reason for Dreyfuss's career change (the transition from stage design to industrial design lasted from 1928 to 1935), the example of his mentor Bel Geddes must have been foremost in his mind. Likewise,

Teague's public declaration that he was abandoning graphic design for industrial design in the summer of 1926 probably added to Dreyfuss's perception that the best minds were leaving these fields for more fertile territory. The one job offer that had awaited Dreyfuss upon his return from Europe in 1928, general supervisor of merchandise design to R. H. Macy & Company, he declined. He rejected the offer because he found that he was merely to provide suggestions to manufacturers rather than having a say about new designs. Later Dreyfuss would routinely decline work when he could not

have ultimate control of the design process. Just two years later, working as a consultant to Bell Telephone Laboratories on their installations of equipment in New York, he rejected their offer of $1,000 to create an "appearance model" of a new telephone with a unified handset for a similar reason: if he could not consult with Bell's engineers on the project, he had no interest in it. In the long run, this demand proved effective: Dreyfuss received credit as the designer of Bell Telephone's 1937 Model 302 telephone. The conditions he set — working on a level of equality with the manufacturer and its employees and collaborating on designs rather than serving as an aesthetic consultant — turned out to be among the most important in his early career.

Dreyfuss's desk at 580 Fifth Avenue, c. 1932. His theatrical flair is shown in this custom-built desk for his new office; hidden levers opened a humidor and liquor cabinet. A drafting board was also concealed inside, as well as a telephone.

Dreyfuss's commitment of service to society, however, had to be balanced against the reality that he was a young man of no means, other than those provided by his wits. Throughout his life, he was realistic about the system within which he operated, and it dictated in large degree his formulation of design:

It is pointless to produce a product so expensive that no one can afford it, or so underpriced as not to permit a reasonable profit to the manufacturer. Good design need not increase cost.[1]

The parameters he set later in his career were repeated so often they became a sort of mantra: safety and convenience of use, ease of maintenance, cost, appeal, and appearance. For Dreyfuss, these five points constituted a road map, not a blueprint, for successful design. It was their prioritization that made his designs exceptional. His five points are all centered on human, not abstract, values.

By 1929 Dreyfuss was hard at work redesigning pianos, glass containers, and household hardware such as hinges, keys, and escutcheons, for various American manufacturers.[2] In 1930 Doris Marks began to negotiate fees for his work that reflected the level of his talent.

While Dreyfuss was not a skilled draftsman in the sense of being able to execute finished engineering drawings for his industrial designs, he had an extensive art background. His exceptional ability to produce work on schedule came from his years of work at the Mark Strand Theatre (he was very proud of having produced an average of a show a week for this vaudeville/movie house for five years). He had developed a technique of working in watercolors that was successful, for example, in rendering costume designs, and he now applied it to the more painstaking work required for illustrating products. While few such design drawings remain (most were destroyed after microfilming in 1948), these early works must have had a significant personal importance to him, for they survived to become part of his gift to Cooper-Hewitt Museum in 1972, the year of his death. The drawings run the gamut from mildly abstract representations of fruit for the Swift Company to the geometric patterns he created for the Hickok Belt Company. Most interesting of these works is a series of label designs he created for the Charles Higgins Company of Brooklyn, well known at this time as a manufacturer of inks and other artists' supplies. Through what may have been an interesting episode, Dreyfuss was called upon to redesign the appearance of the can that contained Higgins Vegetable Glue, a product similar to rubber cement.

A possibly apocryphal story in a 1934 issue of *Forbes* magazine related that one of Dreyfuss's employees wrote to the Charles Higgins Company of Brooklyn complaining about the poor design of the glue's square container after she cut her hand on the rim.[3] (The product was typically scooped directly from the can and spread with the fingers in doing paste-up work.) Supposedly, the firm responded to Dreyfuss that he was welcome to do better. In spite of a number of restrictions imposed by Higgins, Dreyfuss jumped at the opportunity. Higgins dictated that the new design could cost no more to produce than the present one. Furthermore, the name of the product, its mottoes "Strength" and "Sure to Catch," and its lion insignia constituted a trademark that would have to be retained. Also, the design had to maintain the glue's identity as a Higgins product, and any innovations introduced needed to be applicable to the rest of the company's line of products.

Charles F. Higgins & Co., Higgins' Vegetable Glue, before (background) and after redesign, 1932. Dreyfuss experimented with a variety of color schemes and patterns, retaining the heraldic design of the lion in all of these versions. For the final design, the "silver" of the new round can was allowed to show through to create a third color.

Dreyfuss began by changing the square container to a round can, allowing for easy removal of the glue. He turned to historical precedents, specifically heraldic designs, and modernized the emblem of the lion to provide a more striking graphic treatment. In addition, he separated the light-colored upper portion of the can from the darker bottom with a wavy silver line, providing a graphic motif that could be applied to other products. By using the existing silver (actually tin) coating of the container as a design element, he added a third tonality to the palette of light green and opaque white.

The segue from packaging design to product design was not a clear-cut transition for Dreyfuss. An electric toaster, designed for the Birtman Company in 1932, was another early challenge. Sales appeal was again an important aspect of the total design. Dreyfuss's proposal provided a package that acted as a pedestal for display of the toaster in a department store setting and as a handsome presentation box if it were to be given as a gift. The curvilinear form of the box was in fact far more streamlined than Dreyfuss's design for the toaster itself, which retained many of the angular forms associated with Art Deco. The project provides insight into a transitional stage in Dreyfuss's work: integrally cast on the bottom of the toaster's Bakelite base is the notation "style-designed by Henry Dreyfuss." This seems to be the only time this phrase was used, but it accurately describes his role. Dreyfuss's major idea was that the bread should be visible as it toasted. Seeing the toast brown in the Birtman Visible Toaster was not so important, but it helped to persuade customers to move away from the open type of toaster. (Later toaster-ovens with their large glass panels recognized that there are limitations to the degree that automatic control satisfied users.) The range of toaster design schemes in Dreyfuss's proposals to the Birtman Company is very broad, even including a model that can only be described as Cinderella's carriage because of its pumpkin-like form. The model was done in clay, an early instance of Dreyfuss's preference to work with a clay model of a product in order to resolve the proportions of the design.

Washburn Co., kitchen tools before (right) and after redesign, 1934. Dreyfuss not only simplified the patterns of the kitchen tools, sold at five-and-dime stores, but also brought a new color scheme to them. The new designs in this photograph would have had bright canary yellow handles.

Another early, and somewhat unexpected, success was the reshaping of an entire line of inexpensive kitchen tools for the Washburn Company of Worcester, Massachusetts, not just in form but also in color. John S. Tomajan, the organization's president, remembered that an air of humility distinguished Dreyfuss from his peers in early 1934. Tomajan had already visited a number of designers he had read about in a *Fortune* magazine article that same year. He noted, "the general impression I had of the profession at that time was that there was an air of cocksureness on the part of designers."[4] Dreyfuss was different from, and also the youngest of, the designers mentioned in the article. He promised Tomajan only consistency, saying, "Mr. Tomajan, I do not claim to be infallible. You have a widespread responsibility. You have to be concerned with sales, manufacturing, engineering, financing, and, incidentally, design. I spend all of

Interior of William K. Vanderbilt's Sikorsky S-43 amphibian plane, 1936.
Dreyfuss's inspired use of cloud photomurals avoided the ostentation that might
be expected in a "flying hotel" such as this custom-built plane for one of New
York Central's scions. Mrs. Vanderbilt complained that she could not fit her hat
through the entry hatch (above); Dreyfuss's suggestion was that she remove it
before entering.

Cities Service Petroleum Co., customized interior of Douglas DC-2 airliner, 1934.
Hardly spacious by today's standards, the DC-2's interior was amplified by
Dreyfuss's use of linear forms along the roof line and multi-functional seating.
Maps and fold-down tables were elements he would employ again in decades
to come.

had been streamlined — most notably Carl Kantola's landmark sheathing of New York Central's Commodore Vanderbilt around 1932. Innovative new trains like Union Pacific's M10,000 (City of Salina) and Burlington Northern's Burlington Zephyr were treated as totalities on their exteriors (though their "consist," or make-up of cars, was quite abbreviated in terms of what the public expected of a full-service train). Dreyfuss's work on New York Central's Mercury, which traveled the New York–Cleveland route, was seminal. He was solely responsible for coordinating the appearance both inside and out on a major line that provided all the amenities offered by rail travel, the only mode of land travel that could be referred to as luxurious.

The New York Central was feeling the pinch of a contracting economy as well as competition from automobiles and airplanes. Dreyfuss recounted that the project was almost scrapped because the cost of a completely new train was prohibitive. He had given up, it seems, when he took a trip to the country (probably to his house in Kent Cliffs, New York, purchased in 1935) in order to relieve some of the stress resulting from a failed enterprise. Leaving Manhattan, he saw a train yard full of unused commuter cars owned by the New York Central, and, suddenly inspired, he immediately returned to the city. By using the existing stock as the starting point to redesign, he got the railroad's accountants to agree that this strategy could cut costs by 75 percent, and the plans for the Mercury

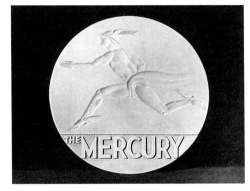

were revived. The debut of this ensemble of modern design in 1936 was widely heralded as a breakthrough in rail travel. By lowering window sills in the observation car, Dreyfuss gave passengers a panoramic view. (Turning passenger seats around to face the landscape rather than one another was, no doubt, as important an innovation.) The Mercury seemed to onlookers to be a single tube of flying gray metal, an illusion aided by a color scheme that unified the appearance of all of the cars and redesigned vestibules to finesse the junctions between them. It was a success with business travelers and the public alike, and it put Dreyfuss and his associate Julian G. Everett in position for what was so far the firm's greatest single success, the all-new, "all-room" (that is, no coach class) 20th Century Limited.

The 20th Century Limited had been in existence long before Dreyfuss began his relationship with the New York Central in 1934. It had been the flagship train of the railroad since its inception in 1902. The train's appeal was not only its facilities but also the unrivaled service it provided to passengers in an age when it was the conveyance of choice for the well-to-do making the trip between New York and Chicago. From the iconic cowling of the engine to the wrappers on the sugar cubes in the dining car, the

New York Central Railroad, emblem for the Mercury, 1936. This is possibly one of the earliest works sculpted by John Amore, who worked with Dreyfuss from the 1930s through the 1960s. The Mercury emblem retains a classicizing quality typical of borrowings from European sources. As Amore was a Prix de Rome winner, this is not surprising.

Above: New York Central Railroad, new Mercury locomotive with J-1c Hudson at Harmon, New York, 1936. This photographic comparison shows the "guts" that lay underneath the streamlined exterior that was Dreyfuss's major contribution to the "new" locomotive.

Top left: New York Central Railroad, Mercury locomotive with its tender at Harmon, New York, 1936. This side view of the locomotive and its tender gives some idea of the coordination of elements that characterized Dreyfuss's design. To contemporaries it appeared to be a flying tube of gray metal. The raised "skirt" reveals the massive disk drivers, which were illuminated at night to dramatic effect

Bottom left: Henry Dreyfuss, New York Central Railroad, detail, Hudson J-3a locomotive for the 20th Century Limited, 1938. This detail of the running gear of Dreyfuss's streamlined locomotive shows the Scullin disc driving wheels and Timken roller bearings that were found as equipment on some of the loco- motives. Their asymmetric pattern and bright applied finish were immortalized in a similar view by artist/photographer Charles Sheeler in his monumental Rolling Power of 1939.

Above: New York Central Railroad, furnishings for the dining car of the 20th Century Limited, 1938. The "chimney" motif found on the menu cover was continued on the ceramicware, matchbooks, and sugar-cube wrappers that Dreyfuss designed as part of this total environment.

Left: New York Central Railroad, observation end, 20th Century Limited, 1938. This publicity photograph shows Dreyfuss's paint scheme, which unified the visual appearance of the 20th Century train. The tailboard sign can now be seen in the Smithsonian Institution's permanent exhibition "Material World" in Washington.

New York Central Railroad, three streamlined Hudson J-3a locomotives photographed at Rensselaer, New York, 1938. Perhaps the most striking locomotive designed during the 1930s, the workhorse that pulled the 20th Century Limited diverged markedly from the "inverted bathtub" form of the Mercury locomotive.

Dreyfuss version of the 20th Century was rivaled only by its exact contemporary, the Broadway Limited, styled by Raymond Loewy and architect Paul Philippe Cret. The two trains made their debuts on the same day in 1938. Like the Mercury, the new 20th Century Limited exposed the running gear of its motive power while exhibiting near seamless form in the thirteen trailing cars, where sheathing of vestibules and pinstriping of the cars carried the theme of continuity even further than the Mercury did. Dreyfuss had specified that lights be installed above the drive wheels so that mechanics could work with ease at nighttime. In fact, these lights were left on all night, adding to the public's sense of awe at the train in motion. The steam evacuating from its huge cylinders also added to the train's atmospheric quality.

While contemporary photographers and artists such as Charles Sheeler were enamored of the train's external forms, a real revolution in transportation design had been wrought in the interiors as well. The dining car was the masterpiece of the train. It contained two small spaces at either end that could be screened off from the main body by glass partitions, creating more intimate dining rooms. These spaces could also be used as waiting areas for travelers coming to dine. The need for waiting, however, was partially obviated by the intertrain telephone system that allowed passengers to call ahead for reservations. The train's logotype — the chimney, as it was referred to by New York Central enthusiasts — appeared on plates, menus, wine lists, and paper ephemera. Travelers would have seen the graphic logo first on the red carpet that greeted them at Grand Central Terminal in New York or LaSalle Street Station in Chicago, and well-wishers would have glimpsed it on the observation car's tailboard as the train departed.

The interiors of the cars were a model of restraint and serenity. Skillful lighting, provided by fixtures newly designed by Dreyfuss in conjunction with the manufac-

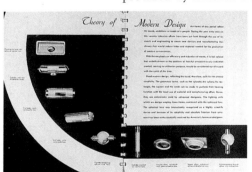

turer, the Luminator Company of Chicago and Plano, Texas, provided a warm blend of general lighting with tightly focused incandescent spotlights. Some of these fixtures contained a second, tiny, red bulb that allowed them to be switched from white to red in the dining car after the dinner service was cleared. Dreyfuss imagined the Café Century, as it was dubbed, as a rolling nightclub, with chinaware in rust reds to complement the color scheme and with long-range radio reception and phonograph records to provide music. Sound emanated from speakers concealed behind photomurals depicting the New York and Chicago skylines. In other cars, contrasting color was used to provide narrow widths with a feeling of greater space, which was emphasized by trough lighting running the length of the cars. Divans and tables broke up what had once been rows of seats. Dreyfuss eliminated the mirrors that typically hung on

Dust-proof construction of this fixture prevents depreciation of light output. The magnifying lens controls the beam to prevent glare. An extra rose-tinted bulb on a special circuit gives a pleasing effect when the main system is turned off after dinner.

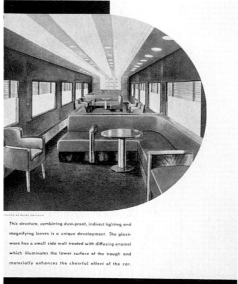

This structure, combining dust-proof, indirect lighting and magnifying lenses is a unique development. The glassware has a small side wall treated with diffusing enamel which illuminates the lower surface of the trough and materially enhances the cheerful effect of the car.

The unusual design of the Observation Section and Lounge affords the opportunity of friendly groupings in an atmosphere of informality combined with dignity. A cove conceals lamp bulbs which are enclosed in dust-proof boxes having diffusing glass covers, providing a moderate intensity of illumination on the ceiling. A Luminator glass unit, equipped with formed-in magnifying lens, has been mounted over each seat and focused at an angle that causes the projection of a high intensity beam on the reading matter. Dust-proof construction assures the continued maintenance of maximum illumination over a long period of time. Control of light beams by the magnifying lenses prevents glare in the eyes of passengers seated across the aisle.

Left and above: Luminator Co., "Radiant Incandescence in the Twentieth Century," publicity booklet, 1938. In this remarkable summary of Dreyfuss's technical innovations in the 20th Century Limited, we become aware of how his concern for stage-lighting techniques translated into his industrial design practice. This booklet also published renderings of the train which are now in the Albany Institute of History and Art, Albany, New York.

Left: Designer unknown, New York Central Railroad, interior of the dining car of the 20th Century Limited, prior to 1930. For comparison with the unified theme established by Dreyfuss in his version of the 20th Century Limited, note the mixture of art deco motifs in one of its predecessors.

Above: New York Central Railroad, interior of club car for the Mercury, 1936. As Dreyfuss noted in *Designing for People*, "The Mercurys have been called a turning point in railroad design. They were the first streamliners done as a unit, inside and out, integrating everything from locomotives to dinner china." The interior of the Mercury continued the machined forms found on its exterior; the central bar seems to echo the driving wheels of the locomotive.

bulkheads in the cars and replaced them with framed reproductions of great paintings drawn from the collection of the Metropolitan Museum of Art, an approach so success-ful with the public that it became a standard feature on many New York Central trains. In the observation car, instrument displays of the train's current speed and the miles elapsed on the trip added a theatrical touch that involved people in the drama of the train trip.

Just as Dreyfuss had wanted the 20th Century Limited to evoke a comfortable vision of modernity in the mind of the public, he wished to create an imagery of streamlined efficiency in his work for Western Union. He took a single element, the standard mes-sage form that was used at the telegraph office, and made it the central motif of the signage and interior of the model office he proposed. Black-and-white photographs can hardly do justice to the impression that the vivid yellow of the forms, echoed in the yel-low stripes in the linoleum flooring, created when complemented by the blue of the

walls and floor. (Dreyfuss felt these yellow dashes evoked the Morse code used by telegraph operators.) On the exterior of the building, the impact was more immediate and dramatic. A contemporary account stated that the massive telegraph form, which read "Western Union Everywhere," seemed to hover over the entrance, an effect aided by back- and diago-nally-lit etched glass, framed by thin strips of aluminum. Inside, the emphasis was on speed and convenience — message forms were stacked in etched-glass containers that also separated the circular desk into four units, defining the user's space. The mixture of direct and indirect lighting put illumination where it was needed most: at the service counter and the customer's fingertips. Even a cursory glance around the office directed the customer's attention to the clock marking "official time." The brushed aluminum hands

Roland Stickney was described as an iconoclast by one of his contemporaries at the Dreyfuss office. He was certainly one of the finest renderers in the business. While hardly outspoken, he was a great practical joker; on one occasion a glazier was summoned to the office only to discover that Stickney had created an illusionistic rendering of a broken window.

of the clock echoed a decorative band of messengers running around the central "col-umn" (which also cast light against the ceiling). The yellow Catalin plastic numbers and dashes of the clock marking the hours and minutes completed a scheme that distin-guished the public areas (blue) from that of the office workers (yellow).[9]

By the second half of the 1930s, a persuasive formal language had been developed by Dreyfuss and his associates Herbert Barnhart (perhaps the first designer he hired), Julian G. Everett, and a master renderer named Roland Stickney. (Stickney came to the office from the world of automotive rendering and, in fact, continued to work for Rolls-Royce on the side.) The stylistic approach of the Dreyfuss firm was applied to any number of disparate commissions worked on by these men. Moving away from the per-fect, streamlined, teardrop forms that dominated industrial design in the early 1930s,

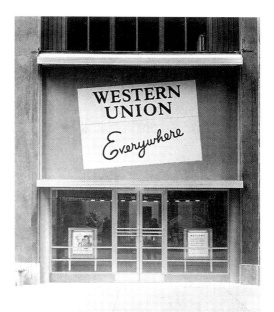

Top: Western Union, model office (exterior), Philadelphia, 1936. Floating above the entrance to the model office was a reproduction of the standard form found in all Western Union offices; its bright yellow color was enhanced by indirect lighting and an aluminum frame that sought to modernize the image of a very traditional company.

Bottom: Western Union, model office (interior), Philadelphia, 1936. Dreyfuss's total control of this environment emphasized efficiency through the effective use of color, form, and material. The blue linoleum floor had inset yellow sections that visually recalled the Morse code.

Dreyfuss's new approach emphasized an abstract play between vertical and horizontal forms that resulted in a convincing imagery of power. This can be seen in a brief survey of the firm's important designs from 1937 to 1940: the Hoover Model 305 vacuum cleaner, the John Deere Model A and B tractors, the cowling of the Hudson J-3a locomotive that pulled the 20th Century Limited, and the lesser known but coeval truck cab for the Federal Motor Truck Company. In all four designs a dominant vertical is balanced by flanking horizontal forms. This aesthetic reached its ultimate statement in the design for the 20th Century's locomotive, which recalls a rooster's coxcomb or the crest of a classical warrior's helmet. This masculine symbol is juxtaposed with the smooth half-sphere of the engine's boiler. In actuality, the boiler stood well behind the locomotive's headlight and the sphere is, in fact, hollow. As was pointed out by automotive designer Strother MacMinn, a Dreyfuss employee in the years immediately following World War II, all four designs were linked by another factor: they all moved. Whether slowly (the tractors) or even back and forth (the vacuum cleaner), they took their cues from the world of automotive styling, where the illusion of "movement while standing still" had long been a desirable goal. (An automobile that is perfectly balanced visually may be admirable, but may lack emotional appeal, which is what sells cars, and probably vacuum cleaners.) Dreyfuss abandoned the strategy of stressing movement, however, when it was suggested by his designers for the revamping of Royal's type-

Caricature of Raymond Loewy's streamlined pencil sharpener, c. 1955. In *Designing for People* this cartoon appears in the margin with no direct commentary. Implicitly Dreyfuss was criticizing the cognitive dissonance created by a streamlined form screwed solidly into a desktop. At least one of Loewy's designs had a "skirt" to conceal the offending hardware.

writer. In relation to early studies, the final design has its share of rounded forms, especially at the corners, giving a subtle message about the quality of its manufacture. But as a stationary object it was designed to sit very solidly and rather squarely on its table or desktop.

Indeed, an obscure but pointed critique of the streamlined designs of Dreyfuss's rival Raymond Loewy is found in the marginalia of *Designing for People*, where Dreyfuss drew a caricature of the famous teardrop pencil sharpener (unaccompanied by any identification) with an overemphasis given to the two screws that mount it firmly to its support.[10] He might just as well have criticized Walter Dorwin Teague's "Bluebird" (also known as the Nocturne) radio receiver designed for the Sparton Corporation in 1934 — as powerful an example of "façadism" as one will find during this period in U.S. industrial design. (The components of the Bluebird are fitted into a small sheet-metal box that bears no relation to the circular blue-glass mirror in front of it.) All of these examples, including those by Dreyfuss, are characteristic of the "classical" phase of the design decade of the 1930s and the reliance on the visual vocabulary of what has been termed the Machine Age. Yet these are consumer items, and, were we to look at other categories — for example, at machine tools — we would find that there is a confluence of approach on the part of industrial designers, apart from style: concern for legibility and placement of controls, horizontal and massive forms giving reassurances of stability and safety, and unification of awkward and dirt-catching forms of subcomponents. In addition, there is something else that industrial designers contributed that engineers had not concerned themselves with: an appreciation that the proper mental state of a machine's operator is as much an aspect of functionalism as is the layout and structure of the mechanism itself.

With the coalescence of the industrial design profession and its working processes in the late 1930s, Dreyfuss turned his attention from the consideration of specific products to their context: the packaging of the product and its replacement parts or accessories, the look of the organization that sold it, and, soon, the packaging of services that were less tangible than washing machines and alarm clocks. In 1936 he noted:

General Electric Co., refrigerating machine type CF-1-B16, 1934. In this breakthrough design, dubbed the "Flat-Top," Dreyfuss modernized the form of the refrigerator and banished the monitor top (GE continued to market the latter after the new machine's debut). Open, the refrigerator reveals a striking band of black plastic with bright metal studs; its thick walls were necessary because sodium dioxide was used as a relatively inefficient refrigerant.

> A second important change in industrial design is the way in which it is branching out into new fields — from the merchandising of clocks, washing machines, stoves, furniture and glass, etc., design is beginning to play a part in the merchandising of such things as railroad tickets, telegrams, gasoline, and business, institutional prestige.... Designers are busy using color, form and materials, concretely to help sell such intangibles ... the designer must be able to understand merchandising and know how to extract the vital principles involved in the problems. These ideas must be dramatized through visual design so that they are intelligible to the average person.[11]

The successful industrial designer was thus involved in abstracting the most important elements found in a product (often its newness) and dramatizing them — an operation analogous to a stage designer's attempts to represent a mood through a setting. At the same time, the product-by-product approach that initially put Dreyfuss in the public eye progressed into a consideration of systems, such as telegraphy and transportation. We have seen this abstraction in the linoleum pattern at Western Union that denoted the Morse code and made it visible, and in the Hudson J-3a locomotive's forms that came to stand for power, speed, and stability.

In a 1934 article targeted at managers of bus transportation services, Dreyfuss wrote that their struggle was one between "Modernism and archaism":

Western Clock Co., four generations of Big Ben alarm clocks, c. 1910–33.
In this classic image of industrial design's impact upon daily life, one sees how
Dreyfuss's redesign of an inexpensive alarm clock brought it cachet by imitating
more expensive luxury items. His efforts at making the clock appear thinner and,
by implication, mechanically superior are readily seen as well.

That it could be made far more interesting to travel by bus rather than by train or private car, that it could be a travel *service* and not merely a means of getting from one place to another, is entirely within the realm of possibility and is certainly desirable. Bus travel needs sales appeal and the bus company which operates a service that invites and attracts, that makes the public want to travel in its buses as the most desirable way of going places and doing things, will lead the field.[12]

Dreyfuss placed his message in a positive context, revealing how the success of design in other realms of transportation boded well for bus services. The specifics he suggests in the remainder of the article relate not so much to such things as color and fabrics that enhance the image of the vehicle or its operator as to the creation of sales appeal on the part of bus com-panies. He is no longer addressing a product *per se* but the packaging of a service. His recommendations to railway operators were similar:

> In designing a train we not only design the train outside and in, but also every detail and accessory including the porters' uniforms, matches, magazine covers, china, silver, etc. We feel that if we are de-signing a product, any detail related to that product in the way of cartons, display, lettering, etc., is part of the job.[13]

Dreyfuss does not make a distinction between the service of transporting people and the marketing of a product. His desire is for the transition to seem smooth and effortless, as if the shift from designing an alarm clock to organizing the appearance of an entire rail line was simply an increase in scale. Speak-ing of design as some amorphous abstraction, he saw it as living protoplasm, engulfing and absorbing inde-pendent entities and growing stronger by doing so:

Westclox, Big Ben alarm clock, 1939. When Dreyfuss updated the Big Ben, once again at the end of the 1930s, the sharp edges of the art deco period had given way to a new cleanlined form. The package the clock came in was also part of the industrial designer's assignment.

"Being of proven value, design is growing, broadening, permeating other fields in which it has not before been tried . . . it is now tackling more extensive and more com-plicated problems."[14] It would be more accurate to say that the Dreyfuss firm was "growing, broadening, [and] permeating other fields." His urge to connect design with the zeitgeist obscures the fact that the progress he celebrates came from the discrete actions of individual men and women. In this passage he does, however, touch upon design's evolutionary qualities: a concern with the modernization of products and with a widening of design's domain. Marketing or creating appeal was key to furthering both tendencies.

Thus the new profession asserted itself in an area that had once been the juris-diction of architects and interior designers. A review of Dreyfuss's architectural and interior designs indicates that, partly as a result of his work designing for the stage, he sought to emphasize the integrated setting rather than rely solely on visual effects. His later interiors were designed to augment and accommodate the drama of human events that transpired within his spaces and were not designed simply according to visual aesthetics.

The 1930s saw the establishment of Henry Dreyfuss's basic tenets of design: utility without sparseness, attention to detail within a comprehensive and cohesive program of appearance, and an emphasis on human use that would grow even stronger. These priorities would continue to guide the work of Dreyfuss's firm in the following decades, but certain crucial modifications would determine the character of his mature work fol-lowing the turbulent period of World War II. Dreyfuss soon restricted his activities to an average of fifteen major clients at any time, all employing him on a retainer basis and ceding responsibility for most aspects of their public appearance to his control. Such a stable and profitable system of operations allowed him the freedom to experi-ment, which simply was not feasible when working on a purely case-by-case basis. This system was linked to the development that most distinguished him from his contem-poraries in the field in the following years: a dedicated pursuit of a rational system of anthropometrics that could complement and guide his focus on consumer comfort, safety, and convenience. The coming decade would find Dreyfuss and his associates facing a series of challenges that would take this line of inquiry from the status of lux-ury to that of necessity. In responding to these challenges, they changed the nature of the practice of industrial design in the United States.

NOTES

1. William F. H. Purcell, "Designing for Heavy Duty: A Study of Functional Design Applica-tion to the Hyster Company," *Automotive Industries* (June 15, 1962) (unpaginated offprint in pro-motional mailings files, Dreyfuss Collection). While Dreyfuss's partner Purcell is the author of this article on their redesign of Hyster's forklift truck, the observation is Dreyfuss's and is expressed, less succinctly, in his writings from the 1930s.

2. In addition, temporary exhibition designs for the Delman Shoe Company, Dennison Man-ufacturing, and Macy's were helping to pay the rent.

3. "New Product Designs Start Stampede," *Forbes* 33 (February 1, 1934), 15.

4. John S. Tomajan to Rita Hart, November 9, 1953, *Designing for People* anecdote file, Dreyfuss Collection, 1973.15.5.

5. Ibid.

6. Ibid.

7. Some confusion is caused by the company's re-use of historic names through the years, but there is no mistaking the earlier Chronotherm (1920s), with its vertical thermometer and round clock face, for Dreyfuss's sleek and unified box of 1938.

8. "Planning for Intensive Use of Space," *Architectural Forum* 64 (April 1936), 238–39.

9. The summary in one article noted: "The effect is dramatic, and the design is also thoroughly sound from a practical point of view. . . . Henry Dreyfuss has made this telegraph office stand out from its neighbours, and competitors, as expressing a service which is endeavouring today to establish itself as something more than an occasional necessity." "Workshops for Minds: A Telegraph Office Designed to Attract Business," *Industrial Arts* [England] (Summer 1936), 104–10. See also "Office for Western Union Telegraph Co.," *Architectural Forum* 66 (February 1937), 119–21.

10. Dreyfuss, *Designing for People* (New York: Simon and Schuster, 1955), 77.

11. Dreyfuss, "What Is Happening in Design," *Electrical Manufacturing* 17 (February 1936), 20–21.

12. Dreyfuss, "Modernism or Archaism in Transportation," *Bus Transportation* (July 1934), 241.

13. Dreyfuss, "Industrial Designing is a Profession," *Electrical Manufacturing* 18 (October 1937), 50.

14. Dreyfuss, "Modernism or Archaism in Transportation," 239.

Crane Co., publicity photograph for the Criterion lavatory, 1951.

Chapter 3: THE 1940S

THE DECISIVE DECADE

THE 1940S OPENED WITH A CHALLENGE for American industrial designers. They had finished celebrating their success in shaping the future at the 1939 New York World's Fair to find that exhibition design was not the growth industry they had expected. The large number of designers gathered under the roofs of Teague, Bel Geddes, and Loewy were unnecessary to the now-leisurely pace of redesigning products. Were the stars of the fair victims of their own success? Hardly. The lingering doldrums of the Great Depression, consumer anxiety over the war in Europe, and a lingering inferiority complex about European sophistication impeded the realization of the "World of Tomorrow" in the United States.

Henry Dreyfuss recalled that on the day Franklin Delano Roosevelt opened the New York World's Fair, the industrial designers had followed the comfort station attendants in the parade of contributors to the fair.[1] It was easy for Dreyfuss to make this comment some fifteen years later, when he was clearly at the top of his profession. But joking aside, the fair had not been without its difficulties for him. Dreyfuss's exhibition for American Telephone and Telegraph (AT&T) had gone well enough, with demonstrations of the Voder (an early electronic synthesizer capable of imitating the human voice) and free long-distance phone calls for those people not averse to being monitored by their fellow fair-goers. But the World of Tomorrow exhibit that he designed had gone less well. Attempts to end the six-minute multimedia event in the center of the Perisphere in "a blaze of Polaroid light" as he had originally proposed proved unworkable. Julian G. Everett, his associate and architect on the project, mentioned to another colleague in later years his own animosity toward Grover Whalen, president of the fair, who continually cut the budget for this exhibit.[2] In a handwritten note, composed at midnight on May 7, 1939, and mailed to S. F. Voorhees, president of the board of design

for the fair, Dreyfuss noted that the night he had visited the exhibit in person his metic-
ulously organized presentation was a cacophony of lighting, projection, music, and
narration all out of synchronization.[3]

The end of the "Design Decade," as the 1930s were labeled by *Architectural Forum* in
October 1940, did not find Dreyfuss decisively the leader of the "Big Four" (or Five, if

one adds Harold Van Doren, in the Midwest, to the list of Bel Geddes,
Teague, and Loewy). Dreyfuss benefited tremendously, however, from a
number of enduring accounts that expanded his purview during this
period: Hoover, Deere & Co., and Bell Telephone Laboratories, among
them. He was beginning to define an approach that was friendly to big
business but still allowed him to criticize the status quo, that was pro-
tective of the consumer without being patronizing, and that was devoted
to an aesthetic of simplicity without the harshness of European formal-
ism characteristic of the middle phase of the Bauhaus (c. 1923–28).
Graphics, corporate identity, and packaging — what may have been separate pursuits for industrial designers during the 1930s — became the
province of a unified design sensibility that stressed evolution over revolution, cleanlining over streamlining, and "survival form" over strict
functionalism.[4]

This period in American design history is not well documented, but
one case is instructive in understanding the difficult situation the industrial designers encountered in the 1940s. Walter Dorwin Teague, Sr., a
member of the board of design for the New York World's Fair since its
inception in 1936, had contributed an astonishing nine corporate exhibits to the fair. Yet the drop-off in commissions once the fair opened
had Teague searching for new possibilities to keep his staff busy. He began undertaking trips to Washington in search of assignments con-
nected with military work and was successful in obtaining military contracts.[5] Dreyfuss,
his competitor, was on a more secure footing during this period. His work for Bell Telephone Laboratories and other major clients increased dramatically as it became clear
that the United States's involvement in the war in Europe was certain.

Dreyfuss's accomplishments in the first half of the 1940s are not well known. He
was among the most important industrial designers involved in the war effort. As his
office manager, Rita Hart recalled, the entire office was reviewed and, with one exception, granted "Q" clearance, the highest security rating accorded civilians.[6] Because
much of the firm's involvement with the war effort involved matters of national security, and were confidential at the time, its accomplishments during this era have never
really been fully evaluated. By the time the projects were no longer secret, they were
passée.

Top: Voder display from AT&T exhibition, New York World's Fair, 1939–40. Voder was an
early voice synthesizer developed by Bell Telephone Laboratories. This was just a part of the
exhibition Dreyfuss coordinated for the Bell System.

Bottom: "Centerton," detail of diorama from the Theme Exhibit, New York World's Fair,
1939–40. Along with his associate Julian G. Everett, Dreyfuss conflated various schemes of
the city of the future that ranged from Ebenezer Howard's "Garden City" to Le Corbusier's
"Ville radieuse." Centerton was to be the nexus of a series of dispersed communities set in a
greensward; it was to be the cultural and governmental hub that made this vision workable.

One interesting, apparently unpublicized, project that Dreyfuss undertook in 1943 was for Henry Luce, editor in chief of all Time Inc. publications. Dreyfuss prepared a lengthy, seventeen-page letter giving Luce his critique of *Time* magazine.[7] In this document he showed tremendous concern that the magazine articulate the political and social differences between the United States and Germany. Dreyfuss was not merely noting these contrasts; he was also telling Luce how to make them sharper and more visually striking for the reader (one suggestion was to illustrate President Roosevelt against a background of Allied flags and Adolf Hitler against a background of massed artillery). In the 1946 prospectus for his autobiography, realized in 1955 as *Designing for*

Dummy cover from letter to Henry Luce regarding *Time* magazine, July 19, 1943. Dreyfuss's goal was "to make *Time* look as interesting as it reads." He revolutionized the appearance of the magazine cover, saying "it is OK to use F.D.R. or Mr. Lindbergh without suggesting their positions in the world — we all know them. But I'd like to see a background of oil wells for Mr. Pew — of a boat for an Admiral. These backgrounds suggestive of the work or interests of the men are often right in the picture — more often they are not, and then must be put in." This determined, ironically, the appearance of his rival Raymond Loewy on *Time*'s cover on October 31, 1949.

People, Dreyfuss referred to the industrial designer as "the artist of democracy,"[8] and surely his conception of this role evolved from such assignments. Dreyfuss also advised Luce to revamp the cover of *Time* to make it more informative to the potential reader by associating the ever-present portrait of the man or woman of the week with symbols of his or her pursuit. It was this presentation that determined the format of both Raymond Loewy's portrait on the cover of *Time* (October 31, 1949), and Dreyfuss's own portrait on the cover of *Forbes* (May 1, 1951).

In this aspect of his work with big business, Dreyfuss needed sensitivity to be able to mediate between self-promotion and self-effacement. While he seldom displayed anything resembling envy of Raymond Loewy's practice, he was heard to remark, "I don't want to be publicized the way Raymond Loewy is, and all that flashy stuff, but I really would like a *Time* cover story."[9] Dreyfuss was circumspect regarding such fanfare. He was also mindful of the conservative attitudes held by his clients. When he did choose a higher profile, following his move to California in 1945, he hired publicist Ben Sonnenberg at the princely sum of $25,000 per year. Both the outlay of funds and the intrusion into their private lives discomforted Dreyfuss's wife. A crucial part of the publicity campaign was a well-placed article in the *Saturday Evening Post* in November 1947, which quelled rumors that the office in New York was on the verge of closing.[10] Dreyfuss played up his involvement with important projects whenever and wherever he could. For example, a *Life* magazine article on the new 500 series telephone in 1949 shows him with Bell Telephone Laboratories President William Martin.[11] A likeness of the designer also appeared in a two-page advertisement for Honeywell heralding the universal adaptability of the round thermostat in 1953.

Dreyfuss obviously enjoyed the respect of his clients — witness his involvement with Washburn Tools throughout the 1930s, the resumption of his work with Crane Company

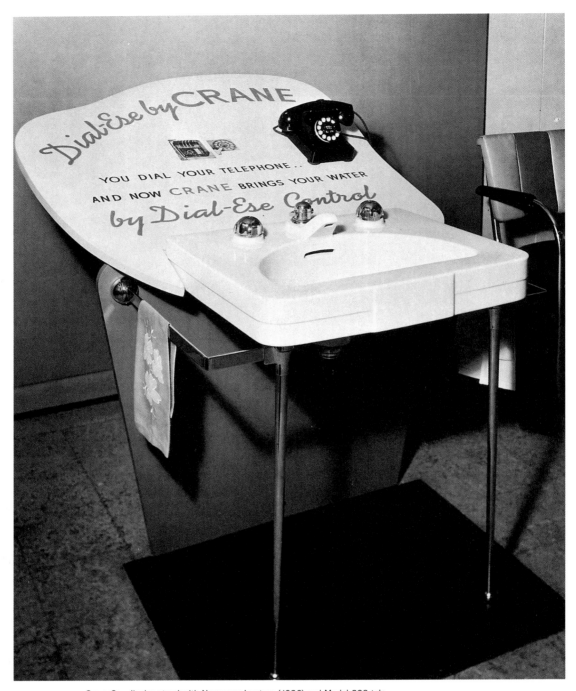

Crane Co., display stand with Neuvogue lavatory (1936) and Model 302 telephone (1937), photographed 1944. Dreyfuss had a predilection for creative
re-use of his own designs. Here he has incorporated two successes from the
1930s into a dealer display of the mid-1940s. Dial-Ese control refers to the
newly designed hardware for the lavatory, which has an integrally molded spout.

Crane Co., Pullman domestic water closet, plaster model, photographed 1944.
Showing Dreyfuss's continuing interest in space reduction in domestic settings,
this Pullman toilet betrays his fascination with geometric shapes and his experience in outfitting passenger cars.

Hoover Co., Model 60 vacuum cleaner, 1940. Almost exactly contemporary with
the Model 305 was the Model 60. It pioneered a different form with a wrap-
around "headlight" which echoed the horizontal bands of the bumper below.
These parallel lines were part of the Dreyfuss cleanlining approach of the
1940s, seen in everything from the interiors of airplanes to record players.

in the 1940s on its line of bath fixtures, and his enduring relationship with Deere & Co. on long-term projects, including the development of a high-visibility compact tractor. Also, his regular updates of the Westclox (by this date General Time) lines of clocks and watches, the new vacuum cleaners he designed for the Hoover Company, and his revised layout of *McCall's* magazine were all part of work quietly pursued during this period. Not all business relationships, however, were successful. For the National Biscuit Company (Nabisco), he proposed new graphic designs for packaging and patterns for their crackers and cookies, but the account went to Loewy. Product, transportation, and

environmental or interior design remained the strongest areas of his output during the 1940s.

Dreyfuss's practical knowledge on how to best display and present information began with such designs as the Socony-Vacuum display at Rockefeller Center in 1934 and 1935 and AT&T's New York World's Fair displays of 1939–40. His ability in this area probably gained him the design project for the Situation Room for the Joint Chiefs of Staff in 1942. The Situation Room, officially Strategy Rooms A and B, built under tight security, was a commission ideally suited to Dreyfuss's abilities. General William "Wild Bill" Donovan of the Office of Strategic Services, the predecessor of the Central Intelligence Agency, was responsible for Dreyfuss receiving the job. While the information conveyed from this office may have been more important to the country than from that of a corporate client, Dreyfuss always considered clarity of presentation a paramount concern.

Given only six weeks to assemble the conference rooms, he had the interiors built in sections at a set design studio in New York. The sections were then reassembled "like a jigsaw puzzle" in Washington:

> [The assembly] constituted the relatively simple part of the problem, however. The real jigsaw puzzle lay in planning, procurement and installation of security devices, soundproofing, air conditioning, a telephone system, several means of still and motion-picture projection, and a complicated lighting system.[12]

Solutions to spatial challenges were found that were nothing short of ingenious:

> The setup was resolved into two large rooms identical in size and parallel in the long dimension, and a small workshop for the preparation of material and storage of maps. Also adjacent was a "file" of sliding four-by-eight-foot screens arranged so that they could be pulled out on tracks. One screen could be used, or a series of screens buckled together, with transparent overlays showing essential data pinned to them.
>
> A world map, accurate and up to date, was painted on a curved, metal-clad surface, twenty-five feet long and twelve feet high, on a wall

Above: Hoover Co., Model 010 dry iron with "pancake" dial, 1947. The focus of this project was on the dial controlling the heat range. Dreyfuss shows an appreciation that function and formal elegance were not antithetical.

Left: Advertisement for Model 28 vacuum cleaner

of one of the main rooms.... A projector was also trained on the map so that slides, when inserted, graphically depicted action anywhere in the world or indicated weather conditions or other desired information. The other room was for projection of 16-mm. motion pictures, still pictures, and drawings.

Emphasis was placed on making the necessary machinery (movie and slide projectors, variable lighting, etc.) as unobtrusive as possible. In a moment of inspiration, Dreyfuss sought out an overhead projector similar to those used in bowling alleys for the display of participants' scores. Curved contours allowed for the mounting of large-scale maps without interruption.

By downplaying hierarchies in the placement of seating, Dreyfuss helped assuage sometimes difficult issues of rank and service in a setting where such matters were best put aside. To create the Situation Room, Dreyfuss drew upon his knowledge both as a theatrical designer and as an industrial designer, with over ten years experience in each field. We begin to understand the significance of his special approach, when he states that "the genius and experience of Hollywood and Rochester [i.e., Eastman Kodak] were called in to help devise the best visual presentation."

Dreyfuss's entrée into the upper echelons of government probably came through Wallace K. Harrison, whom he would have met in the 1930s, during the building of Rockefeller Center, for which Harrison was one of the leading architects.[13] Harrison's connection with Nelson Rockefeller also later led to Dreyfuss's receiving the contract for outfitting the conference room at the U.S. Office of the Coordinator of Inter-American Affairs in Washington. Harrison held several posts in this agency established by Rockefeller in 1941.[14] It was in its designs for the Socony-Vacuum Touring Service Bureau in Rockefeller Center that the Dreyfuss firm experimented with curved and contoured walls, as well as with the kind of gadgetry that became essential in the Situation Room. Publicity photographs taken when the touring service opened show Nelson Rockefeller happily engaged in operating the displays Dreyfuss and his associate Julian G. Everett had designed.[15] Historian Jeffrey L. Meikle has associated the curvilinear forms of the touring bureau's interior with the smooth flow of products within a consumer culture, a "streamlining" to ease sales resistance.[16]

While the codification and application of the Dreyfuss firm's work in anthropometrics and human factors is the province of the 1950s, important antecedents for their development are apparent in the firm's wartime experience and its immediate aftermath. Historians of design have often emphasized the European contribution to ergonomics, or human factors, as it has been dubbed, short for "human factors in engineering psychology," as it has been referred to in the United States. Certain rules of thumb for the design and use of seating and tools existed in Europe during the 1930s, but nothing as extensive or detailed as Dreyfuss's seminal *Measure of Man* of 1959 was available to civilians prior to its publication.

Socony-Vacuum Touring Service Bureau, Rockefeller Center, 1936. Socony-
Vacuum, later known as Mobil, sought to inform the public of its worldwide ties
through this early "infotainment" installation. Dreyfuss was fond of maps for
their supposed objectivity, which, in fact, allowed for formal manipulations that
made them effective in modifying difficult spaces.

Strategy Room for the Joint Chiefs of Staff of the United States Armed Forces, Washington, 1942. The OSS commissioned Dreyfuss to create this least martial of all "war rooms." A crash program saw the interiors fabricated in New York and erected in Washington in a period of less than two months.

Undeniably, the interest in human factors in the operation of machinery resulted from military experiences during the last years of World War II. The origins of these concerns are largely based on the work of psychologists like Paul M. Fitts, who, because of their experience as pilots, worked out problems in cockpit design during the war,

especially regarding the interaction between fighter pilots and their equipment. The high speed of such aircraft had led to increasing numbers of "human errors," many of which proved to be the result of asking for too many responses from the pilot in too little time. Certainly the most crucial realization was that such situations had to be conceived of in terms of a man/ machine system, in which a human subject receives information via displays and takes action through controls in an environment of continual feedback.[17] Probably the greatest and least-heralded advance Dreyfuss made during this period was his recognition that use, most notably of "fitting the machine to the man rather than the man to the machine," was beginning to play a larger role in his working method.[18] The seminal developments pioneered in wartime work concerned the rapid setup and use of carriages for 105- and 155-millimeter guns for the War Ordnance Department and habitability studies of crew interiors for the United States Navy in the postwar years. The accounts of the

research of the "classical period" of human factors development (the so-called "knobs and dials era" that followed on the heels of the war) and the presence of related publications in design engineer Alvin Tilley's files in the Dreyfuss office point to the firm's importance in this area. It was Tilley, hired by Dreyfuss in 1946, who drew the now-famous anthropomorphic charts of Joe and Josephine, Dreyfuss's typical Americans. Tilley was responsible for most of the interpretation of the hodgepodge of information Dreyfuss's researchers presented to him. For example, information on human measurements came not only from military sources but from the fashion industry in Manhattan.

Work accelerated at the Dreyfuss office when the United States officially entered the war. This was due partly to their involvement with Bell Telephone Laboratories, which had many military contracts. Early work on the physical aspects of radar and sonar systems had the firm consulting on airborne and shipboard equipment. During the last two years of the war, consideration about the way people interact with new technologies was no longer a matter of a system versus its operators. A "man/machine

Top: United States Army Ordnance Division, 105 mm/155mm gun carriage, 1942. An analysis of the deployment and setup of this design's predecessor resulted in a reduction from fifteen to three and one-half minutes in the new model. Note wire-frame figure with the scale model of the gun.

Bottom: Bell Telephone Laboratories, AN/ASB radar display, 1950s. This later piece of equipment gives some indication of Dreyfuss's role in wartime development work for Bell Telephone Laboratories.

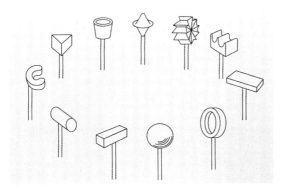

Top (this page): Illustrator unknown, eleven knob shapes distinguishable by touch alone.

Bottom (this page): Douglas Aircraft Corporation, cockpit of Douglas Globemaster transport plane, early 1950s. Accompanying an article on human engineering as it related to business developments, this illustration shows examples of the knob designs in use.

Top right: Consolidated Vultee Aircraft Co., Stinson "Flying Station Wagon," 1947. This popular post-war plane had interiors updated by Dreyfuss as well as added soundproofing. Here was the practical predecessor of the more experimental Convair Car.

Bottom right: Consolidated Vultee Aircraft Co., Model 37 transport plane, rendering by Theodore Kautsky, 1945. Kautsky had previously worked with Dreyfuss on the interiors of the Theme Exhibit at the 1939–40 New York World's Fair. Here in this cutaway of the interior of the massive transport plane we get an idea of why Dreyfuss described the challenge as furnishing "a huge, inelastic pickle or cigar. . . . The only thing the designer can squeeze in is his imagination."

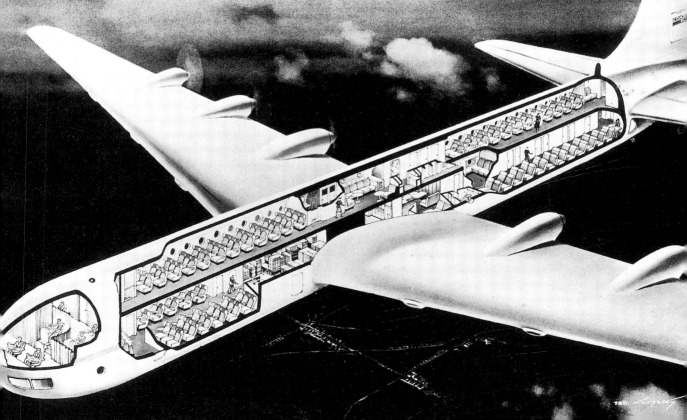

system" with input for a human operator through displays and his or her taking action through controls had become a reality. For example, in designing a radar display featuring a cathode-ray tube, it was not enough to make a durable machine that reported information accurately. Locating controls according to their importance, rather than according to the convenience of the manufacturing process, was critical. Operator vigilance was paramount; for example, simply making a picture tube's display brighter would not solve the problem of eye fatigue. The shape of things became as important as the actions they performed. For example, investigations at the Wright-Patterson airbase in Dayton, Ohio, had determined that there were eleven shapes that could be distinguished by touch alone when mounted at the top of control levers (illustrated on p. 88). This meant that operators no longer had to take their eyes off the displays or views outside their windshields in order to operate controls safely.[19]

Donald Deskey, Shelter Industries, prefabricated house, 1946. Deskey bested Dreyfuss in seeing examples of his design actually produced; nonetheless, the Dreyfuss/Barnes design made better use of the country's massive assembly line capabilities, idled at the end of World War II.

In addition, the Dreyfuss firm was substantially involved in projects intended for postwar production — the most famous of which were undertaken for Consolidated Vultee Aircraft Company. The company was formed in 1943 when Consolidated Aircraft and Vultee Aircraft merged; later it became Convair, and still later part of General Dynamics. William A. Blees, considered something of a maverick in the world of aircraft manufacturing, had risen quickly in automotive sales to become a vice president in charge of the Buick, Oldsmobile, and Pontiac sales divisions at General Motors in the 1930s. By the early 1940s Blees was a vice president and West Coast manager for Young & Rubicam, the advertising agency that handled the Consolidated Vultee account. Irving Babcock, chairman of the board of the new company and a former GM man himself, hired Blees away from GM to head military, commercial, and personal sales at Consolidated Vultee. Blees discarded the attractive but high-priced models the company's Stinson division was planning to market following the war in favor of updating the Stinson Voyager and a similar model with a larger space for baggage marketed as the Flying Station Wagon. Both planes would have interior furnishings, color schemes, and soundproofing worked out by Dreyfuss. Blees's formula would make Consolidated Vultee one of the few personal aircraft manufacturers to realize a profit in the postwar era.[20]

Dreyfuss had already been involved in building interior mock-ups for Consolidated Vultee's transport planes (Models 37 and 39) and with the massive XC-99, the largest transport designed in the pre-jet engine era to be built (with the exception, of course, of Howard Hughes's Spruce Goose). The most exciting aspect of Dreyfuss's work for Blees, however, came in two nonmilitary projects: a manufactured house and a flying car.[21]

Top and bottom right: Dreyfuss and Edward Larrabee Barnes, Consolidated Vultee Aircraft Co., manufactured house, 1947. Part of Consolidated Vultee's attempt to find a transition from wartime aircraft production to peacetime profits, this manufactured house fused the special talents of the designer and his architect collaborator.

The young architect Edward Larrabee Barnes joined Dreyfuss in California to collaborate on a project for a prefabricated house.[22] Although Dreyfuss was active in California in 1943 and 1944, he did not move his family there until 1945. Barnes and his wife, the former Mary Elizabeth Coss, whom he had married in 1944, lived for a time in an apartment over the garage of Dreyfuss's first California home. Dreyfuss brought to the collaboration a fascination with assembly-line processes from his design work for mass production in the 1930s. Barnes contributed an innovative scheme to break up the repetition that often results from building large numbers of houses at one time. He varied the contours of the layout by using an L-shaped patio wall. This allowed the houses to be staggered in relation to one another and thereby avoid the monotony associated with developments like Long Island's Levittown.[23] Dreyfuss, working with engineers, came up with a plan for building much of the plumbing, ductwork, and electrical wiring into prefabricated wall sections, which would then be erected on site. This proposal took full advantage of assembly-line production and reduced the on-site building of the components. The plan also called for a wall section that combined a honeycomb-like paper insulation that was glued to metal panels to provide rigidity with lightness and take advantage of wartime breakthroughs in materials technology. Dreyfuss worked with Barnes's wife, Mary, on color schemes for the interior of the model house.

The project was originally intended to provide employment through the government's Guaranteed Market Program for the large numbers of workers formerly involved in the production of military aircraft. Like many of the prefabricated-housing schemes developed during this period, it did not have a major impact on the postwar housing market. Still, the project's viability concerning consumer acceptance was worked out in greater detail than many schemes, as were its technical aspects. A finished example was displayed to the press in a Consolidated Vultee factory in 1947. In spite of favorable press in such periodicals as *Arts & Architecture*, Consolidated Vultee sold the project to a corporation formed to market the design, Southern California Homes, Inc. It appears that plans went no further than production engineering. Neither of the two prototypes seems to have survived.[24]

Consolidated Vultee Aircraft Co., Convair Car, full-scale clay of Model 118, 1947. This full-scale model of the revised, four-passenger Convair Car was created by Strother MacMinn and Charles Gerry. Their previous experience in the world of custom coach-building in Pasadena was essential to the success of this revolutionary vehicle, which was produced in three fiberglass prototypes.

For comparison, one might examine industrial designer Donald Deskey's completed design for Shelter Industries, which sought to address the problems of cost-efficiency and rapid construction through the creation of a mechanical core, encompassing plumbing, heating, and electrical supply in a single unit that would be fabricated by Borg-Warner Industries.[25] The differences in Deskey's and Dreyfuss's approach to building systems is that Dreyfuss sought to apply mass-production technology to the walls while

Deskey focused on addressing the increasing energy demands and machinery of the modern home (dishwashers, electric water heaters, central heating, etc.). Neither project was as adventurous as that of R. Buckminster Fuller in his postwar Dymaxion House, which was revolutionary in the system of construction and the mechanical core that also served as its main support. Both Dreyfuss's and Deskey's conceptions were unpopular with unionized labor, which saw in such plans the usurping of their domains. The plumbers, electricians, and carpenters whose work would be less necessary to the completion of these houses clearly saw the implications of this type of manufactured housing. This situation is particularly ironic because the Consolidated Vultee house originated from the desire to provide employment opportunities. In any event, political considerations at least partially account for the lack of commercial success in these postwar, mass-produced, housing schemes. Barnes felt that the withdrawal of government support was also to blame for the commercial failure of the Consolidated Vultee project.

Consolidated Vultee Aircraft Co., Convair Car, Model 116, September 1947. Posed with a model of the Convair Car, Model 116, are Henry Dreyfuss, Bill Purcell, Strother MacMinn, and Charles Gerry. MacMinn wrote: "I think that photo was taken in San Diego at Consolidated Vultee ... What I'm pointing to is the all-important nothing that seems to characterize many PR photos ... You should note that Henry, Charlie, Bill Purcell and I all have our sleeves rolled up. This signifies that we're *all* working and directly involved with the subject, not just talking and having our picture took."

Another project for Consolidated Vultee garnered far more public attention. This was the Convair Car, more popularly known as the flying car, a project directed by Theodore P. Hall, chief design engineer for Consolidated Vultee. Hall deserves credit for the idea of the functioning design. The predecessors of the flying car are too numerous to mention, but a working version of the idea was rare. From the limited accounts available, it seems that Hall had developed his concept independently, built a successful prototype, the Model 116, and then sold it to Consolidated Vultee. Ideally, the flying car would provide its users with greater mobility and independence. The Convair Car, unique among such competitors as Robert Fulton's Airphibian, provided separate power plants and fuselages for the airplane unit and its road-going counterpart. It did not have to expend the energy necessary to haul its flight unit from location to location, and had the additional appeal of making it feasible for owners of the vehicles to rent flight units, reducing their initial investment. Salesmen, for example, might own the ground vehicle, rent the flight unit at a local airport, fly several hundred miles to another airport, then use the vehicle alone to drive to their business calls.[26]

Henry Dreyfuss and his team joined the project after Consolidated Vultee decided to produce a more robust, four-seater version, the Model 118, in 1944. A remarkable team was assembled for this effort. Joining Dreyfuss immediately after the war was a talented designer named Strother MacMinn, a native of Pasadena. As a young man, MacMinn had worked for the Walter M. Murphy Company, a *carrozeria* that built the

Strother MacMinn, best known as an automotive designer, worked with Dreyfuss after he established an office in South Pasadena following World War II. His admiration for Henry Dreyfuss continued long after he left his employ. One of the most articulate and knowledgeable educators in the field of automotive design, he is shown here creating a clay model, 1946.

Above: Dreyfuss and Ted Hall, Consolidated Vultee Aircraft Co., Convair Car, Model 118, 1947. This is the four-seater version of the Convair Car during a successful test on April 28, 1948. Note the long, tapering tail of the aerodynamically shaped automobile component.

Left: Dreyfuss and Ted Hall, Consolidated Vultee Aircraft Co., Convair Car, Model 118 with flight unit, 1947. This image captures the most important difference between the Convair Car and its competitors: not having to drag its aircraft component along wherever it went.

bodies covering the chassis of such luxury cars as the Peerless and the Cadillac. MacMinn, a self-described car nut, had worked briefly during the late 1930s in Detroit under Harley Earl at General Motors in the Art and Colour Section (later the Styling Section). He brought to the Dreyfuss office firsthand knowledge of automotive aesthetics as well as the working process perfected at GM. He later passed these skills on to some of the most distinguished figures in postwar automotive design when he was an instructor at the Art Center College of Design in Pasadena. MacMinn worked with an excellent draftsman and model specialist named Charles Gerry, who he said "could draw a perfectly straight line with a 9H chisel-point pencil." Together they coped with Consolidated Vultee's demand that the vehicle be changed from a two-passenger, Volkswagen-like aerodynamic unit to a four-passenger sedan. Working in clay from quarter-scale up to a full-sized version of the car, they prepared the necessary engineering drawings to realize the vehicle in fiberglass, making it extremely light and capable of reaching an astonishing ninety miles per hour, powered by a 26½-horse-power Crosley engine. In short, the resulting automobile was far ahead of its time in terms of its aerodynamic envelope and efficiency. Coupled with a flight unit that boasted a 190-horsepower Lycoming aircraft engine, the flying car, Model 118, was an engineering success.[27]

Alas, this remarkable achievement fell victim to new management and bad press. When Floyd Odlum purchased Consolidated Vultee after the war, he began weeding out unprofitable ventures. Odlum's policies led to a sense of urgency regarding the Model 118's development. During flight trials in 1947, an unfortunate set of circumstances led to an accident that sealed the fate of the project. A team working with the Convair Car had spent many hours testing the flight unit. Satisfied with their progress at the end

of the day, they left the combined unit at the airstrip with its electrical systems disconnected. The next morning, when the flying car became airborne, the pilot was unaware that electricity had not been flowing to the fuel gauge, and thus he had no indication that he was dangerously low on fuel. He soon realized, however, the precariousness of the situation and managed to crash-land the aircraft in the desert. The pilot and his passenger survived, thanks in part to the vehicle's aerodynamic flat bottom, but this prototype was a total loss. Reports of the accident in the press made no mention of the Model 118's air- or even crash-worthiness. Coupled with a limited market for such an innovative system of transportation and the high cost of production, the flying car suffered a quiet death.[28] Hall continued to work with the concept, buying the two remaining vehicles back from Consolidated Vultee. He went on to produce a road vehicle, the Airway. An all-aluminum, compact, two-seater car, it was powered by a 10-horsepower engine and utilized a single-speed transmission with an emergency low gear.[29] This car was clearly an outgrowth of his Convair Car

Bell Telephone Laboratories, "French phone," Model 202, 1927. This photograph of the "French phone" with its original handset shows the awkwardness of its proportions, especially the narrow neck separating the handset cradle from the base.

experience, but it was out of step with the developing trends in postwar automotive design, which favored powerful engines, options like power steering and power brakes, and styling that was more derivative of the look of aviation than of aerodynamic efficiency.[30] Photographs of the Convair Car in flight have captured the imagination of

many young design enthusiasts. Its carryover of the wartime "can-do" attitude into the postwar period is indicative of the aspirations, achievements, and failures in the world of design in the 1940s.[31]

Simultaneously, in New York, a somewhat less romantic but more far-reaching design project was taking shape. Dreyfuss's relationship with Bell Telephone Laboratories (BTL) had begun long before most accounts, including his own, indicate. As early as 1930, on a consulting basis, Dreyfuss had begun submitting to its management written reports on the installation of Bell equipment in a variety of settings. AT&T was responsible for renting telephone units and providing service to consumers. Its subsidiary, Western Electric, manufactured the units designed by BTL. For the most part, Dreyfuss's recommendations from the early 1930s were of an aesthetic nature, stressing the need for unifying equipment designs and creating a cohesive appearance that would reflect the research of the company's engineers. BTL, the research and development arm of AT&T, was taking consumer reactions to its designs very seriously.

Many writers have since discussed the competition that BTL underwrote in the early 1930s when they approached a range of designers to make suggestions regarding a successor to the 202 series telephone produced in 1927. Research by Sally Clarke has revealed that the mechanical failings of the combined handset of the "French Phone" (as the 202 was popularly known) lay behind the urgency associated with creating its successor.[32] Dreyfuss refused to participate in the creation of a new model telephone when he was not allowed to consult directly with BTL's engineers. Later, when proposals by other designers proved unworkable or unpopular with BTL's engineers, Dreyfuss received the commission for the Model 300 (properly the 302), which went into production in 1937. Dreyfuss's formal debt to Jean Heiberg's 1930 design for the L. M. Ericsson Company of Stockholm is readily apparent in the 302's rectangular base and inward-curving upper body. Indeed, the fact that the 302 as it first appeared was available only with a die-cast metal base while the Heiberg design was produced in Bakelite plastic from its inception is a gauge of the relative conservatism of the engineers at Western Electric and Bell Labs.[33] Nonetheless, the 302 was a marked improvement over its predecessor in both form and function.

Top: Jean Heiberg, L. M. Ericsson Co., Stockholm, desk set telephone, 1930. There is some debate as to whether this design or the Siemens Neophone was the first consumer telephone to establish this archetypal format of one-piece receiver and transmitter cradled in a plastic base with a dial.

Bottom: Bell Telephone Laboratories, Model 302 telephone, 1937.

Above: Bell Telephone Laboratories, Model 302 (left) and Model 500, 1949. This publicity photograph from the year the Model 500 made its debut shows the new phone without its aiming dots.

Top right: Bell Telephone Laboratories, two-color Model 500 telephone, c. 1950. Never produced, a plaster model shows a 500 set with a colored plastic shell only. Note the straight cord to the handset.

Bottom right: Bell Telephone Laboratories, Model 500 in color, production model, c. 1953. The 500 set, because it was produced in color, had a clear plastic finger wheel and a coiled cord distinguishing it from its 1949 predecessor.

Dreyfuss received the go-ahead for the development of a new telephone design from BTL in 1946. According to Dreyfuss's partner Bill Purcell, Robert H. Hose (Purcell's brother-in-law) was hired by Dreyfuss after a meeting in which Hose presented alterna-

tive conceptions of the new desk-set model, referred to as the 500. Hose went on to head up the Dreyfuss effort, and the new design was put into production in 1949.[34] When the 500 first appeared, consumers had their choice of color, as long as it was black (as Henry Ford might have put it, for like Ford's Model T, the speed of the production lines limited any possibilities of a choice).[35] The designers knew that colored plastics would eventually be used but were unable to get the uniform color range and durability they wanted from the materials available in 1949. There are sketches and even a photograph of a two-color model

that preserved the black dial and handset with a colored shell; these date from the period between the 500's debut and the introduction of color around 1953. When colored phones became available, all elements were color coordinated, save for the finger wheel and plungers which disconnected the set; these were clear plastic. Color even came to the cords, which were now coiled instead of straight.[36] The 500 type, as it first appeared, had a black body and a black dial, with the numbers and letters on the outside of the dial rather than under the holes in the finger wheel, as was the case with its predecessor. This allowed the user to read numbers and letters while a finger was still in the hole. The metal finger wheel was painted black.

At first, inexplicably, the dialing speed of customers using the new telephone in simulations was slower than that of the previous 302 model. This led to considerable consternation on the part of BTL's engineers. John Karlin, the first human-engineering psychologist in this country to be employed in private industry, became involved in the project at this juncture.[37] Joining BTL in 1945, Karlin had extensive experience with telecommunications equipment from working under S. Smith Stevens, one of the founders of the field, at Harvard University. Their experiments on the intelligibility of spoken messages under a variety of conditions had far-reaching implications and, as with improvements in aircraft cockpits, had been spurred by the war effort.[38] One of Karlin's earliest tasks was to evaluate the new desk-set telephone design in terms of consumer use and acceptance. Since people rented telephones as part of AT&T's service

and did not own them, in retrospect it seems quite progressive of AT&T to have taken consumer preferences as seriously as they did. Karlin soon realized why users were having difficulty in matching their previous efficiency in dialing with the new design. Moving the numbers and letters of the dial to the periphery improved their legibility,

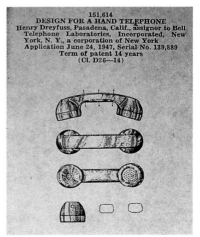

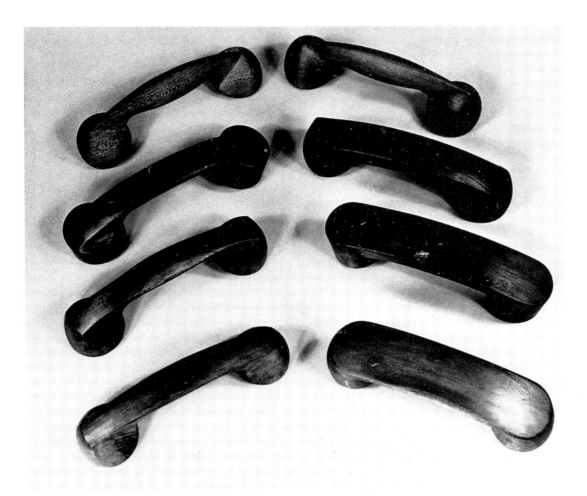

Above: Dreyfuss, handset prototypes in wood showing development of Model G handset for Bell Telephone Laboratories, 1946.

Top left: Bell Telephone Laboratories, early sketch of Model G handset, c. 1947, 1949 publicity photo. While not identical with the handset as produced (notice, for example, the triangular section of this design near the pencil's tip, upper left), these are the general outlines of the world's most prevalent handset.

Bottom left: Bell Telephone Laboratories, Model G handset, design patent, 1948. The bottom row of drawings in this design patent (number 151,614) shows the "lumpy rectangle" of the handset's section, which made it comfortable to hold.

but people had difficulty telling when the finger wheel had stopped moving because it was black against a black background. He suggested placing white dots beneath the holes in the finger wheel, and subsequently the addition was made. Dreyfuss later claimed that Karlin had found that adding the "aiming dots" decreased dialing time by seven-tenths of one second.[39]

Bell Telephone Laboratories, 500 series multi-line set, 1950s. The base of the existing 500 set had to be lengthened to accommodate this row of push-buttons as they were referred to in pre-digital dialing nomenclature. Keeping the proportions sound was a challenge that probably went unnoticed by most.

The "combined set," as the 500 series was called, was composed of the sculptural shell covering the components of the apparatus, a neoprene-coated fabric cord, and what has come to be referred to as the Model G handset. The previous handset had been triangular in cross-section along its handle, with the narrow section at the top, which meant that it couldn't be held against the user's shoulder to free both hands (the user's mouth also ended up too close or too far away from the transmitter for speech to be intelligible). The new handset's section was referred to by the design team as "the lumpy rectangle" because of its mongrel (nongeometric) form.[40] When Dreyfuss first encountered the new handset in a conference with Purcell, he stated that it gave him "griptophobia" and slammed it down on its base, cracking the base model. Purcell assured him that this was exactly what they were looking for, a design that would provide a firm, flat surface for just such abuse. The telephone company's biggest concern was for what it termed ROH, receiver-off-hook situations. Breaking the connection completely and reliably was a major consideration.[41] The design for the Model G handset was completed in the summer of 1947, well before the design for the base. A design patent was assigned on November 2, 1948. The same handset is still used in most public telephones in the United States today, partly because of its resistance to vandalism. The handset's thick section, a result of the manufacturing technology of the time, makes it extremely resistant to abuse.

The designers' intention regarding the sculptural shell of the Model 500's base was concisely summarized by Alvin Tilley in 1953:

Data for the handset preceded the combined set to such an extent that they were almost designed separately, with only a germ idea in the minds of some for the forms tying together. The first form conceived by HD for the new combined set underwent many alterations but it was basically the same from start to finish. It was called the "shoeform" by the staff. All external surfaces were convex with optical cambers to reduce its apparent size. The predecessor was basically an upper section of four concave walls superimposed over a rectangular base. Hence the original conception was the logical outcome of three of our axioms: 1) simplify form, 2) if it is circular make it square, and if it is square make it round, and 3) a design that is neither concave nor convex and without sex is the darndest thing![42]

Above: Bell Telephone Laboratories, Princess telephone, 1959. Another subtle change was added to the Princess after its debut: the inset "panel" provided a finger grip, allowing it be carried in one hand.

Right: Bell Telephone Laboratories, automatic card dialing set, 1962. According to the press release that accompanied this photograph: "Henry Dreyfuss, noted industrial designer, said the new automatic card dialing telephone may someday put the words 'sorry, wrong number' right out of the English language and telephony."

Thus the formal inspiration for the 500 was in part due to its predecessor, the 302; the square base with its classical molding in the 1937 version became a rounded, slightly "bulged" form in the 1949 model, and the "fat triangle" of the Model F handset became the "lumpy rectangle" of the Model G. This summary makes the process sound extremely easy. In fact, modelmaker John Amore was producing so many subtly different versions of the "shoeform" that a new process had to be used to create large numbers of identical plaster models that were then customized to hundredths of an inch. As the summary below notes, the language used to note these changes could be pretty dry:

> Note model #140 to include built-up front corners add to this model a skirt and ¼ inch high feet like model #98, otherwise the same as #103. Combined set C-42-185, 5¼″ wide, with optical corrections and 7 degree rear. Combined set B-42-192-1, 5⅜″ wide, 26 degree dial angle, concave number ring.[43]

The 500 series was tremendously successful in providing a starting point for bringing new services and convenience to users. Multiline sets, automatic card-dialing sets, wall telephones, and mobile phones were all spun off from its basic makeup of components and forms. Even the Princess, the first telephone marketed by AT&T on the basis of style, had its origins in the 500's development (its internal components were almost identical with the 500 except that it had no internal ringer). Its formal development began with the desire to align handset and base in the same plane. Intended as a bedside telephone, the Princess was the first AT&T product to be targeted at a specific market — teenage girls. This stylistic sensation was soon being used in situations that the designers had not anticipated, such as offices. In fact, its base was so light that it sometimes moved under the force of dialing the phone, and many a Princess was pulled off of a tabletop when its cord reached the limits of its stretch. The design solution in this case was to add a concealed metal weight in the base.[44]

The number of 500 series telephones produced is astounding: from an initial shipment of 86,000 units in 1950 the figure mushroomed to 7,184,000 in 1965 for the desk unit alone. These units were clearly among the most numerous objects of a technological nature ever shaped by one person's aesthetic. In total, between 1950 and 1982, 93,412,000 units of the 500 desk set were produced, and the total number of permutations including wall sets, key (TouchTone) sets, and general-purpose sets including the desk model comes to a stunning 161,679,000.[45] During a collaboration that lasted almost three decades, Henry Dreyfuss never lost sight of his role as a surrogate for the eventual user of the telephones and systems he helped to design. His role was to anticipate consumer concerns about how these modern necessities would fit into their

Bell Telephone Laboratories, 500 sets in color with packaging. Color brought in an underappreciated marketing angle to telephones, even though there had been colored sets of a sort as early as the candlestick design. Extension phones are marketed here through the addition of boxes with playful graphics that make them appear similar to other consumer products, even though they were rented as a part of the service.

existing environments, whether they would demand more of the user's attention than previous models, and how they made people feel about a vast communications empire that they usually related to only through these design objects. His "five points" — safety and utility, maintenance, cost, quality, and appearance — served as a guideline for his designs but were not a blueprint. The interpretation and prioritization of these points have made his designs endure. Sometimes overlooked because they now seem old-fashioned, these telephones are entirely representative of their respective eras and of the best that these decades had to offer. Their quiet message of quality was a reflection of the man who helped to shape them.

NOTES

1. Dreyfuss, *Designing for People* (New York: Simon and Schuster, 1955), 200.

2. Julian G. Everett to Raymond Spilman in a taped interview of 1978, conveyed to the author in a telephone interview with Spilman, March 27, 1992.

3. In his letter, Dreyfuss urged Voorhees to see that someone would be hired to keep the equipment in order. "Theme Center — Democracity" folder, file box no. 45, section C.10, New York World's Fair 1939–40 Archives, Manuscripts Division, New York Public Library.

4. On the legitimacy of streamlining in design and Dreyfuss's neologism "cleanlining," see Dreyfuss, *Designing for People*, 77. About "survival form" he wrote: "Designing for today and tomorrow the contemporary designer must express first the utility of the object on which he is working, second the era in which we live, and last, when the design permits, lurking in the background, some form to be remembered from the past that will unconsciously make the consumer more comfortable in accepting what may be a radical new form to him." Dreyfuss, "Book on Industrial Design 1946," *Designing for People* misc. files, Dreyfuss Collection.

5. Dorwin Teague, interview with author, January 21, 1993.

6. Rita Hart, interview with author, April 22, 1996.

7. Dreyfuss had previously done the same for *Life* magazine in 1938. Client response files, Time/Life folder, Dreyfuss Collection.

8. Dreyfuss, "Book on Industrial Design 1946," *Designing for People* misc. files, Dreyfuss Collection.

9. Donald Holden, interview with author, February 20, 1991.

10. Alva Johnston, "Nothing Looks Right to Dreyfuss," *Saturday Evening Post* 220 (November 22, 1947), 20–21, 132–39.

11. *Life* 27 (December 12, 1949), 67.

12. Passages quoted on the Situation Room come from Dreyfuss, *Designing for People*, 162–64.

13. Wallace Kirkman Harrison (1895–1981) was a member of the team properly referred to as the Associated Architects: Reinhard & Hofmeister; Corbett, Harrison & MacMurray; and Hood,

Godley & Fouilhoux. Between 1932 and 1940 this team was responsible for the first phase of building at Rockefeller Center. Raymond Hood's death in 1934 effectively elevated Harrison to the top position as the liaison with John D. Rockefeller, Jr., and Nelson Rockefeller. Harrison's marriage to Ellen Hunt Milton in 1926 brought him into the Rockefeller family circle (her brother David had married John D. Rockefeller, Jr.'s daughter, Abby).

14. Dreyfuss and his team had also collaborated with Harrison and his partner André Fouilhoux on the interior of the Perisphere at the 1939–40 New York World's Fair. Dreyfuss noted the following in his "Brown Book," his compilation of personal projects, under 1942: "Strategy Rooms for Joint Chiefs of Staff (for Gen. Wm. Donovan)." Rita Hart recalled a visit from Donovan to the Dreyfuss offices, interview with the author, April 22, 1996.

15. Most of these displays sought to entertain the public while informing them of the superiority of Socony-Vacuum's process of production, resulting in, for example, lubricating oil with fewer impurities, which were anthropomorphized as the bad elements of society. Rockefeller is shown manipulating a marionette with a control located in front of a display cabinet at the exhibit. Socony-Vacuum, uncatalogued microfilm reel, Dreyfuss Collection. On the business begun by John D. Rockefeller, Sr., see Daniel Yergin, *The Prize: The Epic Quest for Oil, Money, and Power* (New York: Simon and Schuster, 1991).

16. See Jeffrey L. Meikle, *Twentieth Century Limited: Industrial Design in America, 1925–1939* (Philadelphia: Temple University Press, 1979). For more on the subject of streamlining and its relation to the consumer and the human body, see Ellen Lupton and J. Abbott Miller, *The Bathroom, the Kitchen, and the Aesthetics of Waste: A Process of Elimination* (Cambridge, Mass.: MIT List Visual Arts Center, 1992).

17. For an introduction to the history of the development of human factors research and applications in the United States, see Paul M. Fitts, "Engineering Psychology and Equipment Design," in S. S. Stevens, *Handbook of Experimental Psychology* (New York: John Wiley, 1951); Fitts, "Engineering Psychology," in Sigmund Koch, *Psychology: Study of a Science* (New York: McGraw-Hill, 1963); Walter F. Grether, "Engineering Psychology in the United States," *American Psychologist* (1968), 743–51; John A. Kraft, "A 1961 Compilation and Brief History of Human Factors Research in Business and Industry," *Human Factors* 3 (December 1961), 253–83; E. C. Poulton, "Engineering Psychology," *Annual Review of Psychology* 17 (1966), 177–200; Paul G. Ronco, "A Bibliography and Overview of Human Factors Reference Works," *Human Factors* 5 (December 1963), 549–68; and F. V. Taylor, "Human Engineering and Psychology," in Koch, *Psychology*.

18. For the earliest published statement on the Dreyfuss office's approach, see the article written by his partner Robert H. Hose, "Designing the Product to Fit . . . Human Dimensions," *Product Engineering* 26 (September 1955), 166–72.

19. Francis Bello, "Fitting the Machine to the Man," *Fortune* 50 (November 1954), 137.

20. "Stinson's Flying Cars," *Newsweek* 30 (August 4, 1947), 76.

21. It was on the flying car project that Dreyfuss began collaborating with Dr. Janet Travell, who was critical to the development of many postwar projects, making major contributions in the

area of seating in transportation design. Travell, a physician who specialized in injuries of the muscular and skeletal systems, had been introduced to Dreyfuss in 1944. For the story of how Travell and Dreyfuss came to be collaborators, see her autobiography, *Office Hours: Day and Night* (New York: World Publishing Co., 1968), 286 and following.

22. Dreyfuss had solicited recommendations from Walter Gropius, then at Harvard, who suggested Marcel Breuer's student Barnes.

23. Edward Larrabee Barnes, telephone interview with author, February 5, 1991.

24. Henry Dreyfuss and Edward L. Barnes, "House in a Factory," *Arts & Architecture* 29 (September 1947), 31–35, 49–50; "A Quality House Designed for Quantity Production," *House and Garden* 77 (March 1940), 124–26, 181; Edward L. Barnes, "Defense Housing," *Task* (New York) 2, 1941.

25. Shelter Industries document and photograph folders, Donald Deskey Collection, Industrial Design Archives, Cooper-Hewitt, National Design Museum; Jeffrey L. Meikle, "Donald Deskey Associates," in David A. Hanks and Jennifer Toher, *Donald Deskey: Decorative Designs and Interiors* (New York: E. P. Dutton, 1987), 121-56.

26. In a promotional brochure for the flying car published by Consolidated Vultee in 1947, it is referred to throughout as the ConVAIR Car. Folder 1, Consolidated Vultee, Industrial Design Clients, Dreyfuss Collection. For the Convair Car's predecessors and competitors, see James R. Chiles, "Flying Cars Were a Dream That Never Got Off the Ground," *Smithsonian Magazine* 19 (February 1989), 144–62.

27. Strother MacMinn, interview with author, November 24, 1990.

28. MacMinn estimated that, even in optimistic scenarios, the automobile component would cost more than the entire assembly's original estimate of $6,000. Consider, for example, that the top-of-the-line Cadillac for 1953 cost only a few hundred dollars less than this figure.

29. David Burgess Wise, *The Illustrated Encyclopedia of the World's Automobiles* (Secaucus, N.J.: Chartwell Books, 1979), 70.

30. A sad note was added to the flying car's story when a second version of the vehicle was lost in a fire at the San Diego Air & Space Museum (now the San Diego Aerospace Museum) in 1978.

31. For contemporary reports on the Convair Car project, see "Designed for the Air-Minded Autoist," *New York Times*, November 17, 1947 (Dreyfuss Collection); "Long Journey Home: Convair Car Runs Out of Gas," *Architectural Forum* 87 (December 1947), 14–15; "New Aircraft: Close-up of Convair Car," *Aviation Week*, April 19, 1948, 21. For more recent overviews, see John Wegg, *General Dynamics Aircraft and Their Predecessors* (Annapolis: Naval Institute Press, 1990), 184, 186–87; Joe Stout, "GD Flashback: Flying Car Was Designed for Salespeople," *General Dynamics World* (May 1986); Ted P. Hall clippings file, San Diego Aerospace Museum Archives. The last three references were provided by Ray Wagner, archivist at the San Diego Aerospace Museum.

32. Sally Clarke, "Consumer Demand and Bell Labs' French Phone," unpublished paper, Shelby Cullom Davis Center, History Department, Princeton University, Princeton, N.J., April 28, 1995.

33. Kathryn B. Hiesinger and George H. Marcus, *Landmarks of Twentieth-Century Design: An Illustrated Handbook* (New York: Abbeville Press Publishers, 1993), 121.

34. William F. H. Purcell, interview with author, March 16–17, 1991. It is unclear whether Hose was acting as a consultant or as an employee for BTL just prior to being hired by Dreyfuss.

35. When the Model T began to be produced in staggering numbers in 1913, the only paint that would dry rapidly enough to accommodate the speed of assembly-line production was black.

36. Colored plastic bodies for the 302 had in fact been produced during the early 1940s, but were a rarity. See Kate E. Dooner, *Telephones: Antique to Modern, a Collector's Guide* (West Chester, Penn.: Schiffer Publishing Ltd., 1992); Ralph O. Meyer, *Old-Time Telephones: Technology, Restoration, and Repair* (New York: TAB Books, 1992).

37. Bruce L. Hanson, "A Brief History of Applied Behavioral Science at Bell Laboratories," *The Bell System Technical Journal* 62, no. 6 (July–August 1983), 1573; John Karlin, interview with author, August 18, 1995.

38. One notable project that matured in the 1950s was SIBYL, which allowed researchers to test subjects' reactions to the time lag caused by transmissions relayed by satellite, long before such satellites were operational. Its first tests were on rotary versus push-button telephones. Hanson, "A Brief History," 1578.

39. John Karlin, interview with author, August 18, 1995.

40. This and the following quotations are taken from Alvin Tilley's interoffice memorandum summarizing the design effort, dated May 1953, and found in the *Designing for People* misc. files, Dreyfuss Collection.

41. Without visiting the residence or business where the phone was located, the telephone company was unable to determine in these circumstances whether equipment was out of order or if the handset was simply off the hook.

42. Alvin Tilley, interoffice memorandum, May 1953, 1.

43. Ibid., 3.

44. This may have led designer George Nelson to recall incorrectly at Dreyfuss's memorial service that this had been the case with the Westclox Big Ben alarm clock; see "Henry Dreyfuss 1904–1972," *Industrial Design* 20 (March 1973), 42. One might recall Dreyfuss's surprise at a customer's choosing a heavier competitor over the Big Ben in Dreyfuss, *Designing for People*, 68.

45. Program Planning Report A-2402, 1-2, AT&T Archives, Warren, N.J.

Royal Typewriter Co., rendering of proposed typewriter by Roland Stickney, 1944. Among the largest of the surviving works by Stickney executed for the Dreyfuss office, this typewriter is notably "cleaner" than the model that was actually produced. It appears that Dreyfuss often proposed designs well in advance of what clients might accept: this may have allowed him additional room in later negotiations. Stickney came from the world of automotive rendering and worked with Dreyfuss from the 1930s through the 1950s.

Plates

PRODUCTION   OF
THE MERRY WIVES OF WINDSOR
COSTUME FOR SIR FALSTAFF
PLAYED BY OTIS SKINNER
1927

Henry Dreyfuss.

Costume design for Falstaff, *The Merry Wives of Windsor*, 1927. This watercolor
study, one of several from the production, provides a good idea of Dreyfuss's
artistic abilities. From one of his first jobs after leaving the Mark Strand Theatre,
the sketch shows how he used contrasting colors and saturation to build up
outlines. Such works were challenging to him, but he was well served by art
courses taken at the Ethical Culture School.

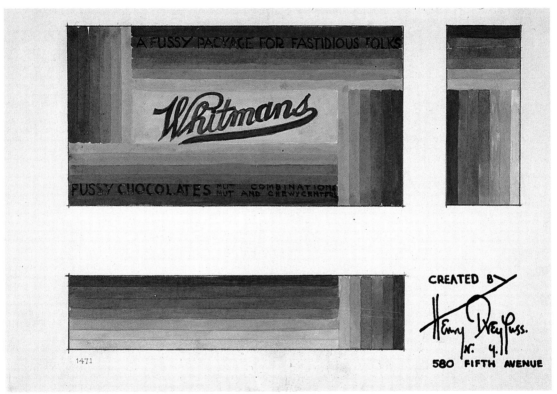

Top: Charles F. Higgins & Co., proposed label design for Higgins' Vegetable Glue, 1932. In a number of such sketches, Dreyfuss experimented with a variety of color schemes and patterns, retaining the heraldic design of the lion in all versions.

Bottom: Whitman Candies, package design, 1930. Dreyfuss claimed in later years that he executed packaging designs only in conjunction with products. The initial years of his practice, however, saw packaging playing a large role in his success. In this refined and geometricizing design for chocolate nut candies, Dreyfuss has included, perhaps tongue-in-cheek, the inscription "A fussy package for fastidious folks."

Top: American Thermos Co., thermos carafes, 1936, 1939. In *Designing for People*, Dreyfuss implied that the form of this desktop accessory was inspired by an ancient Greek jug in the Metropolitan Museum of Art. Often cited as an example of his tendency toward classicism, it was in fact one of dozens of designs that ran the gamut from the bullet-shaped to the spherical. The original model (left) was equipped with a glass stopper; after numerous complaints of breakage, a metal and rubber stopper was substituted (Dreyfuss's suggestion of a hinge was not implemented).

Bottom: Birtman Electric Co., Chicago, Birtman Visible Toaster, Model T-34N, 1932. One of Dreyfuss's first mass-produced industrial designs, this toaster is impressed on the underside of its base "Style-designed by Henry Dreyfuss" with a reproduction of his distinctive signature.

Design for *McCall's* magazine. Henry Dreyfuss was responsible for the design and layout of *McCall's* magazine from 1932 to 1944. His conception was for "three magazines in one," with each section set off by a separate cover.

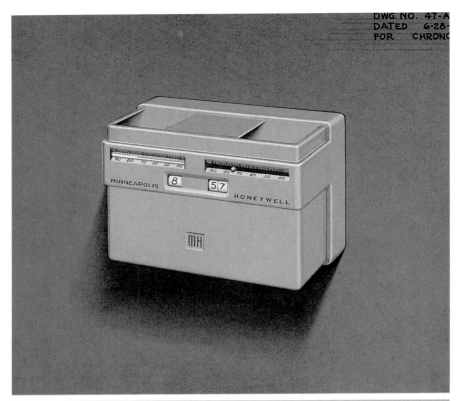

DWG. NO. 47-A
DATED   6-28-
FOR   CHRONO

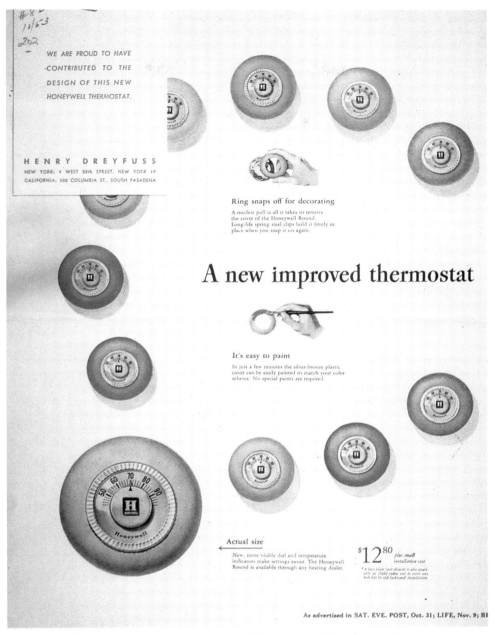

Above: Honeywell, advertisement for the introduction of the T-86 thermostat, 1953. As Honeywell's marketing head recalled, Dreyfuss's notion of making it possible to paint the T-86 to match various interiors enabled color to be used effectively.

Top left: Minneapolis-Honeywell Regulator Company, rendering of proposed thermostat (Chronotherm) by Roland Stickney, 1938. This rendering should be compared with the others from this period illustrated on page 53. The Chronotherm was to be the top of the line in Honeywell's domestic heating controls; Dreyfuss's frustration with the frequent inability of installers to hang them squarely on the wall may have led him to propose a round version.

Bottom left: Minneapolis-Honeywell Regulator Company, rendering of proposed round thermostat (Acratherm) by Roland Stickney, 1942. The genesis of the Round thermostat included name changes as well as alterations in its physical appearance and components. Prototypes and test models of the early 1940s incorporated curved thermometers.

"Has your bath the well-groomed look ?"

As faultlessly groomed as its owner, this Crane Bathroom reflects modern beauty combined with the practical efficiency of the latest in bathroom fixture design.

Your present bathroom can be remodeled to bring you this new attractiveness, and greater convenience. Of course, if you are building a new home you will want Crane plumbing throughout.

Crane offers a complete line of fixtures for bathroom, kitchen and laundry in a wide range of styles—priced to meet every budget.

Shown here for example are the Diana Lavatory, Oxford Toilet and Criterion Bathtub in warm Sun Tan, one of the attractive Crane colors. Crane fixtures are also available in gleaming white.

The shining chromium plated *Dial-ese* faucets operate at a finger's touch. Water pressure has been harnessed to aid in closing, hence wear and consequent dripping are reduced.

Your Crane Dealer will gladly assist you in selecting the Crane fixtures best suited to your needs. His skilled installation will assure you years of trouble-free service. The Crane Budget Plan is available for your convenience.

Two booklets—one on bathrooms and kitchens, the other on choosing the correct heating system—are available. Write for them if you are interested.

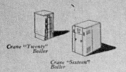

CRANE

CRANE CO., 836 S. MICHIGAN AVE., CHICAGO 5, ILL.

PLUMBING AND HEATING · VALVES · FITTINGS · PIPE

NATION-WIDE DISTRIBUTION THROUGH BRANCHES, WHOLESALERS, PLUMBING AND HEATING DEALERS

BETTER HOMES & GARDENS, OCTOBER, 1948

Crane Co., advertisement featuring the Oxford toilet, Diana lavatory, and Criterion bathtub. All fixtures illustrated in this advertisement were designed by Henry Dreyfuss.

The *Magic Carpet* rolls out again

IT'S Century time! A minute ago, outside the station, you were in the heart of a great city, with crowds, blaring taxis, newsboys shouting the evening headlines. Now you're in a different world as you follow that crimson carpet down the platform of Grand Central Terminal toward the softly lighted, streamlined cars that will be your club on wheels for tonight.

RELAX BY TWILIGHT
Magically, the day's tension vanishes as you step into the Century's Observation Car. Easy chairs invite you to relax. And outside the wide windows, the twilight beauty of the Water Level Route unrolls a background for repose.

THE FACE IS FAMILIAR
There is a fascination about your "dinner of the Century." For nearby may be a face you last saw in technicolor, or one that would be news on any financial page.

AWAKE REFRESHED
You arrive at your best. For all night, in the quiet privacy of your room, a spacious bed, a rubber-foam mattress, and the smooth Water Level Route have conspired to give you deep, refreshing sleep.

The *only* all-room extra-fare train between New York and Chicago.

NEW YORK CENTRAL SYSTEM

20TH CENTURY LIMITED

NEW YORK CENTRAL
The Water Level Route—You Can Sleep

"The Magic Carpet rolls out again," contemporary advertisement for the 20th Century Limited, 1948. This ad serves as a reminder that, whether one rode the 1938 or 1948 version of the 20th Century Limited, Dreyfuss had designed both, as well as the crimson carpet that was rolled out to greet passengers in New York's Grand Central Terminal or Chicago's LaSalle Street Station.

Top: Bell Telephone Laboratories, Model 500. This example, produced in 1955, was purchased from Bell when they offered to sell rental equipment to subscribers in the 1980s. The 1955 model was updated with modular phone plugs and a new handset embossed "AT&T" at a later date. The clear plastic finger wheel and clear plastic plungers (not seen) were introduced when color was added to the line in the 1950s.

Bottom: Bell Telephone Laboratories, Trimline telephone set, 1968. This unusual telephone in clear plastic incorporated flexible circuitry that curved to meet the outline of the handset. One of the few Dreyfuss objects in the Museum of Modern Art's Design Collection, it was the outcome of a search for a "unified handset" telephone by BTL that began in the 1950s.

Bell Telephone Laboratories, 500 series wall telephone, second version, 1956.
Note this improved wall phone's contoured housing with "shoulder creases,"
which allowed the handset to be hung from the side. This was Don Genaro's
first design for the Dreyfuss office.

Above: Henry Dreyfuss, proposed tractor for Deere & Co., 1940, rendering by Roland Stickney.

Top right: Deere & Co., color study for John Deere tractor, 1959. A rough sketch of a color and materials scheme for the New Generation of Power, from the year prior to its introduction.

Bottom right: Deere & Co., control panel for unspecified tractor, 1962. Even after the introduction of the new line in 1960, refinements were continually being made to the new tractors. In this rough sketch, we can see alterations in the color scheme and changes in manufacturing processes.

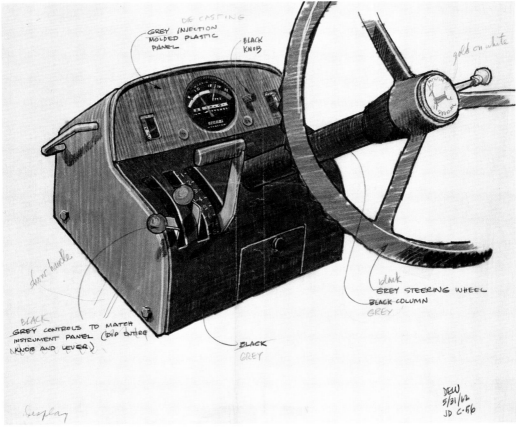

Above: Cover of brochure for Bankers Trust Headquarters Building, 1962. The color themes Dreyfuss used throughout the Bankers Trust Headquarters are shown here as swatches. At the lower right is the Dreyfuss-designed logotype for Bankers Trust from the same period.

Left: Polaroid Corp., Automatic 101 Land Camera, 1964. A less expensive version of its revolutionary predecessor, the 101 also allowed for the use of fast developing black-and-white or color film. Clearly seen in this photograph are the well-marked controls that guided users through the steps of operation. A flip-up viewfinder was held in place by a magnetic catch.

Forbes magazine cover, May 1, 1951. Dreyfuss appears here surrounded by many
of his most notable designs. This image was appropriately aimed at the business
community rather than the general public. Characteristically Dreyfuss is dressed
in brown and is in the process of speaking.

Honeywell, Round thermostat, this version 1964. Perhaps the most ubiquitous piece of domestic hardware in the United States, this design made its debut in 1953. Updated in 1960 to celebrate Honeywell's golden jubilee and modified again in 1964 to accommodate central air conditioning, the durability of the Round in stylistic terms remains unsurpassed.

Chapter 4: THE 1950S

HENRY DREYFUSS, MAN IN A HURRY

THE 1950S SAW HENRY DREYFUSS'S CONCEPTION of industrial design reach millions directly through products such as the Model 500 telephone and the Honeywell Round thermostat. He found himself a leader in his profession, successful in dealing with corporate clients and in articulating the possibilities that industrial design presented to society.[1] The development of an industrial design practice in the office of Henry Dreyfuss, however, cannot be addressed through an examination of his work alone. We have seen that Dreyfuss developed artistically and arrived at a theoretical stance regarding industrial design. Now we need to consider the working methods practiced in the firm he headed. That Dreyfuss's approach evolved can be seen through his "five points":

> The approach — the intelligent approach to any industrial design project is to take the five points that are the catechism of a good industrial designer. They usually are a surprise to manufacturers. They are amazed about it because so many people feel that we are just interested in what a product looks like. That is a consideration, but it is not the first consideration. The vital factors are first, convenience of use, including utility and safety; second, ease of maintenance; third, cost of manufacture and distribution; and fourth, merchandising and competition. And last, but not least, we consider appearance.[2]

Only a few years before there had been only three points:

> Convenience of use
>
> Ease of maintenance
>
> Ease of manufacture[3]

Bill Purcell noted that Dreyfuss loved the idea of being able to sketch the points out on the fingers of one hand, a quick and easy graphic.

Well, you know why he came down to five? Because he used to draw the hand to show it; each finger got a title! . . . To hell with it if they were six! Henry was a wonderful mixture of loyalty to reality, but when he got a human interest thing, like drawing a hand, instead of a list of things, one under the other, he would do that and cheat, make it come to that. That's the innovative mind.[4]

In his maturity, Dreyfuss was a prototypical "design manager" rather than an industrial designer in the sense in which this professional label is used today. Like his contemporaries Bel Geddes, Teague, and Loewy, Dreyfuss stood at the apex of a hierarchy where the cultivation of client relationships was of greater importance to the success of the firm than the day-to-day progress of the efforts of design teams. For this first generation of American industrial designers, selling the client was the most exciting part of the job. Niels Diffrient, who came to Dreyfuss from Eero Saarinen's office and was later a partner in Henry Dreyfuss Associates, has the perspective of a second-generation American industrial designer:

> . . . judging from what I've seen of Loewy's work, and Bel Geddes's work, and Teague's, I think that they were used to the flourish, and it was drama, it was high drama to them, and they played it like the theater. And they wanted to be stars in their own rights. And when the star era began to wane, I think they all generally lost an interest in it. And of course they loved the accomplishment of snaring a big client, and landing a big client was really the thing they were out to do.[5]

This aspect of the profession is of primary concern to the history of design, as these "Big Four" designers were admired by contemporaries as much for their skill in selling design services to major clients as they were for the designs their firms executed. What

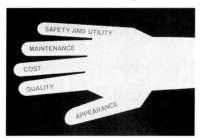

set Henry Dreyfuss apart from these men was the tight aesthetic control he maintained over the designs executed by his office over the course of forty years. Dreyfuss personally approved every design that left his office, a claim that has not been made for any of the other three designers. He balanced his excitement for the acquisition of business with a self-imposed restriction, limiting the total number of accounts to what he could oversee personally. Even then he felt the strain on his time as he shuttled between the California and New York offices. When in New York, he lived at the Plaza Hotel, where he redesigned the Persian Room in 1950. Besides flying coast to coast he also visited clients, logging hundreds of hours on prop-driven airplanes:

> From the outset, I determined to keep our staff small and compact, so we might render a personal service to our clients. As a result, we have restricted our client list to approximately 15, sometimes less, depending on the magnitude of the jobs. If this figure seems small, it should not be interpreted to mean that we have time on our hands. On the contrary, our offices are beehives. The explanation is that some of our clients may

Above: Persian Room, Plaza Hotel, New York, 1950. The press release accompanying this photograph stated: "this new interior combines the best of ancient
Persian and modern interior design . . . twinkling incandescent lights, woven into
soft fabric, surround the guests. Samarkand with wattage." Dorothy Liebes
designed the remarkable custom-woven draperies.

Left: "Five points" illustrated in the form of a hand, Dreyfuss Collection.
Dreyfuss's five points are visually linked here to the conception of counting on
one's fingers; this makes it seem as if the business of industrial design was
easily learned. In fact, the lessons of the 1950s proved that there was a growing divergence between the practice and the public's awareness of it.

Cities Service Petroleum Co., executive plane interior, 1956. Twenty years after his first executive plane interior for this company, Dreyfuss designed this new, multi-functional flying board room. At the same time he was revitalizing their corporate image with new packaging, graphics, and service stations.

each produce more than 100 products a year, or request us to oversee the design of products made in as many as 20 factories or may have us designing a fleet of transport planes simultaneously.[6]

Dreyfuss liked to say that industrial design entered the domestic scene through the back door — via the kitchen and the bathroom. Dreyfuss the design manager, however, always aimed for the boardroom. The outfitting of a Cities Service corporate airplane interior, for example, eventually led to the Dreyfuss firm redesigning the corporation's

entire image during the 1950s. Dreyfuss was persistent: in 1930 he proposed packaging designs for American Safety Razor. From 1960 through 1968, his firm was retained by the company to rework its line of products, including the design for an injector razor that won a "Design in Steel" award in 1962. Thirty years of pursuing a client had finally paid off. In the so-called golden age of industrial design, the Dreyfuss firm was the only one employed by all of its clients on a retainer basis.[7]

Maintaining aesthetic control over the firm's output was a primary challenge for Dreyfuss. His talents usually went where they were most needed: in the guidance of other designers, beginning with rough working sketches often made by Dreyfuss in close negotiation with clients. Not a draftsman in the technical sense, Dreyfuss did execute sketches, renderings, and packaging schemes during the first years of the firm's existence. He was fairly skilled in handling watercolors, but soon left the day-to-day visual development of projects to others, especially Julian G. Everett, whose architectural training had prepared him in a variety of drawing techniques.[8] Dreyfuss used a shorthand sketching style throughout his career to illustrate his concepts for more skilled draftsmen to work up. This style resembled his marginalia in *Designing for People.* Rather than cultivating draftsmanship, Dreyfuss learned to draw upside down in order to impress clients. His wife, upset by designers discarding colored pencils before they were used up, bought pencil holders for the office. When the designers showed a reluctance to adopt them, Dreyfuss began carrying the stubs in his jacket pocket and perfected a technique whereby cupping a stub in his hand and drawing in broad motions over a sketch pad, he hid the sketch until it emerged in completed form.[9]

Donald M. Genaro, who persuaded Dreyfuss to let him join the firm as its first "coop" student and then later headed Henry Dreyfuss Associates, described Dreyfuss as an idea man, capable of immersing himself in details when necessary, and a "quick study" in a number of areas. Work that called for a lot of concentration on Dreyfuss's part could prove exasperating for his employees when there were other decisions, on other projects, to be made. While definitely not a nuts-and-bolts man, he could follow the details of most engineering arguments. The office staff tried to avoid getting him bogged down in details, because he was usually the only one in the office (with the

Top: American Safety Razor, injector razor in stainless steel, 1962. Winner of the "Design in Steel" award in the year of its debut. The design was described as "a blend of a sturdy surgical instrument with a piece of quality flatware."

Right: "Designer drawing upside down," from *Designing for People*, 1955. In a sort of self-portrait, Dreyfuss shows here a talent he perfected: the die-hard showman astonishes a client, who watches as a new design takes shape before his eyes.

exception of Doris Marks) who knew where the organization was headed in a general sense. It was more important for him to concentrate on the overall picture because he was the only person capable of framing it.

Genaro said that Dreyfuss could visualize a total picture in a way that seemed almost mystical. In imagining an interior, the color scheme and overall layout would come to him quickly, much as it had for his stage design. Genaro's description of these cases suggested that Dreyfuss approached states of reverie in which he could visualize something as a totality far more rapidly than anyone else in the office. Dreyfuss, it seems, had thought the same was true of his mentor, Norman Bel Geddes, whose imagination he recalled was prodigious:

> He once told me that he needed a blank wall opposite his desk. It represented the unknown, the untried, the realm he loved most to stare into. It was his crystal ball. Such an imagination demanded boundless courage. He had the audacity to step through that blank wall into worlds where no one had dreamt of setting foot. And he had no fear that people would scoff, though many did.[10]

Dreyfuss managed the business part of the firm with the able assistance of a core team that consisted of Rita Hart in New York, Katherine (Kay) Bray in Pasadena, and, of

Henry Dreyfuss: man in a hurry

course, Doris Marks. After interviews with contemporaries and designers who worked for Dreyfuss, it is clear that his wife freed him from many of the concerns he might otherwise have been burdened with: such things as personnel, billing, and client contracts. She remained outside of the design process in the office itself, but she and Dreyfuss were a team nonetheless; Henry Dreyfuss, the firm, was *their* business. While difficult to document, their relationship was crucial to the functioning of the firm. Without his organizational support team, Dreyfuss could not have maintained the schedule that made him a "Man in a Hurry," as one U.S. Steel advertisement described him.[11]

Henry Dreyfuss and Doris Marks were attentive to their privacy outside of professional matters. Yet many clients were also family friends. When their personal and professional worlds intersected, confidentiality was as important to them as it was in their own family's affairs. Dreyfuss routinely sent letters, clippings, and drawings to friends, and they are kept by many people as personal mementos.[12]

In 1950, when he was written up in the financial section of the *New York Times*, Dreyfuss was a dynamic forty-four years old.[13] Teague was a very mature sixty-seven; Bel Geddes, whose star was fading, was ten years younger than Teague, as was Loewy, who would outlive them all. For another eighteen years, the Dreyfuss firm remained in the front rank. Dreyfuss ultimately exercised control, shaping the team that remained when he "retired" at the end of 1968. They were William F. H. Purcell, his partner since 1946, Niels Diffrient, James Conner, and Donald M. Genaro, all of whom came to the firm in the mid-1950s. Their achievements as Henry Dreyfuss Associates after

January 1, 1969, while considerable, cannot be fully explored in this discussion. Dreyfuss's office was always kept small, around thirty people in New York and fewer than ten in California.[14]

Dreyfuss, in spite of the buttoned-down image that he projected to the business community, was a creative man who sought new techniques in stimulating the design process. Early on, he had stressed the importance of bringing all division heads from a client firm together for initial sessions in a roundtable approach. An early cartoon by Dreyfuss shows a two-headed industrial designer attempting to listen to all of them at once. As his firm grew in size, he used a similar tactic with his own designers and staged think tanks. Designers and nondesigners from the office, usually people not directly involved with the account, would be pressed for new approaches that those more familiar with the challenge at hand might have ignored or discounted. The "outside point of view" that he had emphasized as critical in the design process was sought in his own office.[15]

The visual component of these verbal sessions came with the assembly of "boards," on which were pinned the publicity photographs, brochures, and advertisements generated by the competition. Designers in the office referred to a "visual logic," in which the important areas for consideration would emerge from the welter of such material. This was different from "research" because it was not a considered, but an intuitive, approach that stressed an immediate reaction.

> Well, we always put up all the competition boards. We'd get everything we could on the competition, mainly from the brochures and stuff that the company would have, and we were great believers, all of us were believers in what we called "visual logic." Visual logic was *not* that process by which you thumb through a report and read about things, but one in which you would take all the data and applicable information and pin it up on the wall, and visually scan it, and see what would register as important and not important. And of course we learned such things as who were the big sellers, and we studied them to see why they were better than others, and we'd read all the specifications on something like a tractor, and see what it did. . . . You couldn't come right out and say, "Henry, that's a crummy idea," you know. You had to say, "Uh-huh, uhn-uh," so you didn't tell him it was a truly lousy idea. But at least he did foster creative sessions. Of course, those of us sitting around were just pushing with all we had to try to be the one that had the idea that was best, you know. And so it did encourage some innovative thinking. And oftentimes we would come up with some good things that way.[16]

Henry Dreyfuss was a man of few and carefully measured words when it came to the weightiest matters in managing his staff. His ability to shift and become relatively outgoing in creative sessions serves as an assessment of the range of his abilities.

Left: "Henry Dreyfuss: Man in a Hurry" [U.S. Steel advertisement] *Industrial Design* 7 (October 1960), 19.

Right: Dreyfuss sketching electric ranges for Waste King, 1959. This unposed portrait shows Dreyfuss at work before the "boards," sketching ideas in his cartoon-like style while discussing the work of his competitors.

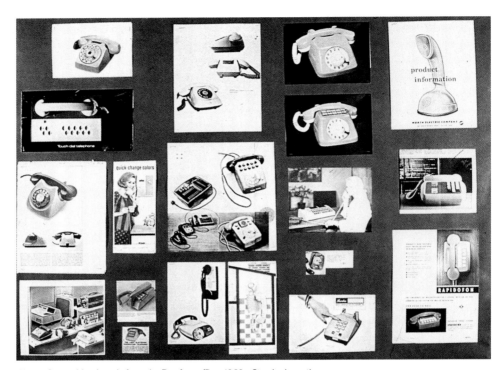

Above: Competition boards from the Dreyfuss office, 1960s. Standard practice
in Dreyfuss's office, as in many others, was to assemble materials on all competitors prior to beginning work on a new design. Here in the initial stages of what
would become the Trimline phone, one can clearly discern L. M. Ericsson Co.'s
Ericofon of 1956.

Right: Photograph of Don Genaro at competition boards, 1960s. Genaro is
shown here pointing to the most admirable of Singer's competitors, Marcello
Nizzoli's Mirella sewing machine for Necchi of Pavia, Italy (1956).

Unlike some of his contemporaries, Dreyfuss exercised, albeit infrequently, his right to veto design decisions by even his top-level staff. A simple comment such as "that's not

Henry Dreyfuss taking sewing lessons with an unidentified instructor, 1960. Dreyfuss prided himself on mastering the skills needed to operate the equipment he designed. Here he is sewing a shirt on a Singer sewing machine.

our office" from him would be understood by those versed in his style as a command to drop that specific approach or design.[17] When it came to assigning projects, a simple pushing of a stack of sketches across his desk to the person he wanted working on the assignment was deemed sufficient evidence that the assignment of responsibility had been made. Conversely, a presentation might be rejected in just the same way, with the visual and written material headed for the floor unless the person making the presentation grabbed it.[18]

He could be equally efficient when it came to making his expectations understood. Jim Odom, who worked for Dreyfuss before moving on to Honeywell where he runs a department of industrial design, related a story from when he was a junior member of the office:

Henry, for all of his success, was a fairly modest person, not given to excess in life style or demonstration. He could quietly devastate a junior designer with an understated remark about lack of attention to a request he had made earlier — I being the devastated party in several instances. On one occasion I had not followed up on an idea he had suggested, and he asked . . . later at my drawing board (he never forgot that sort of thing) if I had done as he had asked. I made several excuses as to why I had not, and he just turned and walked away. After lunch that same day, he came back to my desk and tossed a copy of *Message to Garcia* next to me and said, "Read that!" Which as you probably know is the classic, fabled account of someone who was asked to perform a very difficult task and then proceeded to do it without asking how or why or how difficult it might be or making any excuses. I didn't let Henry's softly stated wishes go unanswered again.[19]

Dreyfuss educated himself regarding products and processes where his clients were involved. He learned, for example, to sew when working for Singer. (As there were no other men in his sewing class, he had to use a tailor's dummy while other students paired up to make garments for one another.) An urban dweller, he learned to operate tractors when Deere & Co. became a client; later he kept one at his home in South Pasadena. He learned to type when designing for Royal and rode in tanks (stateside) during World War II — this he promptly reported to his children in a one-page, hand-drawn "newspaper" he called *The Rinkydink Gazette*.

Just as he found the time on airplanes to clip articles from magazines to pass on, with notes attached, to friends and clients, he took the time to document his work both publicly and privately. First issued in 1939 as *Ten Years of Industrial Design*, a series of privately printed books of his designs was updated in 1947, 1952, and 1957.[20] They went to clients, libraries, and advertising agencies, among other places. For his family,

Dreyfuss assembled travelogues, drawn in colored pencil, "abstracted" from hundreds of photographs taken with a miniature camera. These pictures might document elements as specific as the place settings and centerpiece at his table on the maiden voyage of the S.S. *Independence,* one of Dreyfuss's most impressive efforts from this era. He gives the impression of a man constantly in motion, at work even when pursuing pleasure. Not a "workaholic," Dreyfuss seems rather to have been a man immersed in his role, almost as an actor, delighting in mastering the nuances of his performance.

As convincing as he might have been to outsiders, Dreyfuss left those closer to him with the perception that he did enjoy a certain distance from his assumed persona, "the man in the brown suit."[21]

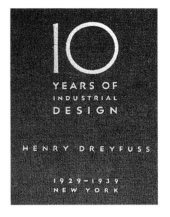

> He was an imposing figure, tall, handsome and immaculately attired. On entering the boardroom, where we usually met . . . he had the personal presence to seemingly dominate the scene and challenge others to question his work. I'm sure he recognized this asset as a sales tool. He made the most of it. You could readily think Henry arrogant but happily, in my view, this was only his front.[22]

Still Henry Dreyfuss was a man deeply enmeshed in his work and in his mission. Herbert Bissell of Honeywell, the author of the previous description, went on to write:

> He was a dignified gentleman of integrity and quite willing, with those whom he respected, to make changes that did not violate his standards.

One of the most revealing and unguarded statements Dreyfuss made about his approach was recalled by his partner, Bill Purcell:

> So he had, coming up that way [through the theater] . . . got a lot of self-confidence. In fact I wonder that he didn't get more, because later, when we traveled, we'd talk a lot, and once I asked him how he felt about going into all these firms and talking to people, selling this idea. We were just going in to someone who had kept us waiting quite a long time, and I said, "Henry, what do you figure you're going to say first to them? What do you say to yourself? How do you think just before you go in, what kind of a plan?" And he said, "I just walk in saying, to myself, you bastards, you bastards, you bastards."[23]

There was, in fact, an adversarial element to his approach with new clients based in the reality that many considered what he had to offer them a luxury. Thus the tight control he maintained throughout his career over initial presentations, with his insistence on presenting a single, well-crafted idea, and only ceding control to his associates once the client was committed, seems perfectly understandable. As one person recalled, when you hired Henry Dreyfuss, you were not hiring an industrial designer so much as you

Cover for *10 Years of Industrial Design, 1929–1939,* 1939. The first of five privately published accounts of Dreyfuss's industrial design activities, this book was one of many mailed to potential clients, press contacts, advertising agencies, and personal friends.

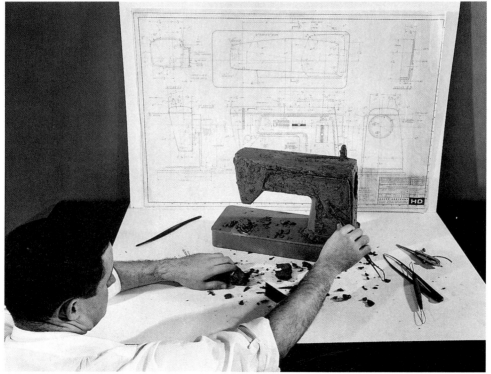

Top: Store for Singer Co., Boston, 1964. Dreyfuss was responsible for Singer Shops Standards Program, begun in 1962, which unified the company's visual appearance in its retail stores. Fusing the straightforward qualities of modern architecture with a playfulness seen in other works from the 1960s, the influence of the young members of the firm was taking on a new visibility.

Bottom: Singer Co., clay model of "New concept Zig-Zag machine," 1960s. Working from an engineering drawing, a member of the Dreyfuss office proceeds in a time-honored fashion to sculpt a three-dimensional model from automotive modeling clay.

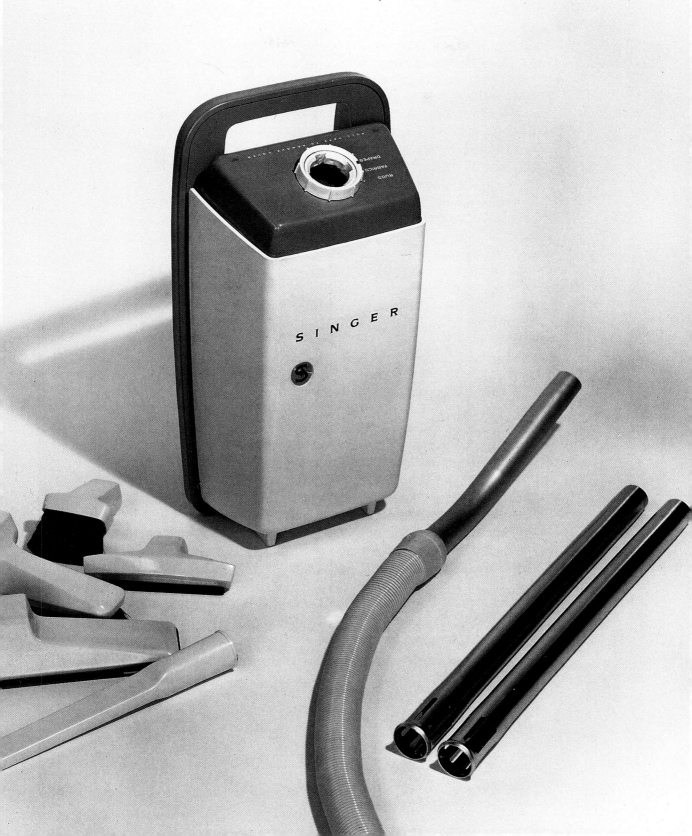

Singer Co., canister-type vacuum cleaner, 1964. Even in the 1960s, cleanlining as a leading conception of design was still a major force in Dreyfuss's aesthetic. One looks in vain for visible screws, inappropriate joints, or nonsculptural forms. Yet in spite of its generic appearance, this suction cleaner in no way echoes his earlier work for Hoover.

were hiring the man and his sense of integrity; he repeatedly described his goal as creating designs that would reflect the integrity of their manufacturers. As his daughter, Gail, put it, "I think there was such integrity, that people . . . knew that if it was going to be able to work, that Dad would be the one who could make it work and would give everything to it, too."[24] Mildred ("Connie") Constantine, a curator in the Department of Architecture and Design at the Museum of Modern Art during its formative years, gave a pointed assessment of Dreyfuss's place among his competitors. After an international design conference in Tblisi in the Soviet Union, where several of the American attendees were not offered the opportunity to speak, an informal conference was arranged in a hotel room by one of the officials:

> . . . the man from the design conference didn't want it held any place where it could be bugged. Well, this was 1968. And we had the most fantastic conversation, give and take, each one of us was able to speak, and ask and answer questions all over the place. And it was better than that whole conference. But there it was very clear that Henry and George [Nelson] were carrying the banner, and in similar ways and in different ways. Because they were both men of integrity, and dignity. . . . And that moral underpinning I don't think existed in a Teague or a Deskey or a [Gilbert] Rohde or certainly not in Raymond Loewy.[25]

Nelson, probably the most articulate writer on design working in the United States during the period from the 1930s through the 1970s, recounted at a memorial service for Doris and Henry Dreyfuss that

> we fought a good deal. I guess I fought with him. I don't think he really fought back very much. It was like a little puppy yapping at a great, well-organized, well-balanced dog. But I did disapprove of him. I disapproved of him because I envied him greatly. And I disapproved of him because he was always taking the corporate side in any argument. And I disapproved of him because he didn't do real far-out "Bauhausy-type" designs.

But Nelson found that his own "purity" regarding design changed as he became more involved in the difficulties of managing the creative aspects of a design firm, especially during the vagaries we now would label as the break-up of modernism:

> . . . surprisingly, these many, many things that we see in our houses and our offices that Henry had something to do with have stood up very, very well. Even that almost invisible little thermostat you see everywhere. It's quite hard after ten years to figure out what you would do that would be any better. As time went by it became clear that Henry was not kidding around. He was a bit of an actor and he came by this honestly and he was very conscious of his impact on other people and he got a lot of fun out of playing this up to the hilt until it got to be a habit. But he never really fooled around with any of these assignments and he never took them on as some of us have done as a convenient opportunity to . . . build a monument to ourselves. This is why a lot of the far-out stuff doesn't look quite as good these days and Henry's looked [sic] very, very solid. . . . I realized the

absolutely extraordinary thing about this man was that he was all of one piece. And the Latin word that has to do with all of one piece I think is called "integrity."[26]

In many ways, this tribute from Nelson is more compelling than many others because these two men, in the years following their deaths, have come to stand for the best that the two camps they represented had to offer. Nelson, who through his writing and savviness in marketing, raised furniture design in the United States to the level where it could legitimately be discussed in the same breath as fine art, represented a segment of the American intellectual community that could be classed as Europhile and architecturally centered: Dreyfuss, perpetually concerned with "what is American about American design," represented a group of commercially oriented improvisators who felt that the torch had been passed from the old world to the new in the 1930s.[27] The battlegrounds ranged from the galleries of museums to the pages of local newspapers. The ironies of this opposition were revealed in strongest relief in the "Good Design" shows organized under the auspices of the Museum of Modern Art in New York and the Merchandise Mart in Chicago, where it has been noted that at one 1951 show "a sterling-silver jug designed by Johan Rohde for the Georg Jensen Silversmithy was, at $210, equivalent in price to the washing machine designed by Henry Dreyfuss for the Hoover Company shown that same year."[28] We are left to contemplate what modern design consists of, in the broadest sense. Can formal designs for a wealthy elite legitimately be compared to the machinery necessary for modern living? Can we consider twentieth-century design apart from the post–World War I notion of "design for the masses"? Such questions were not lost on Nelson who, erudite, well educated, and highly articulate, was in a very strong position (vis-à-vis Henry Dreyfuss, a man with a high-school certificate but a great deal of practical experience) to place his arguments before the public. His recognition of Dreyfuss's ability to operate in this realm of sometimes conflicting standards must be understood as an accolade of the first order.

The "almost invisible little thermostat you see everywhere" (which had been in production for twenty rather than ten years at the time of Nelson's speech) provides an opportunity to explore the complexities of creating a successful commercial design during the 1950s. To appreciate the intricacies of this process, we first have to recognize that the development of the Round thermostat took place over thirteen years and included a number of technical setbacks and a hiatus caused by World War II.[29] Its history borders on mythology, and most of the key players are no longer alive. The Honeywell thermostat is probably one of the most easily recognized and numerous mass-produced designs of this century, and yet its authorship seems disputed. Like much industrial design from this time, the story of its creation is "messy" in the sense that participants did not always keep records or evidence of the contributors to team efforts. The design process is rarely linear, and many product designs resulted from the desires of marketing and sales departments. Nonetheless, it seems that Henry Dreyfuss's role was critical in the success of the Round. He enjoyed the esteem of Honeywell's management as well as its staff, and this new piece of apparatus illustrates perfectly his conception of the role of design in society.

By the late 1930s, Dreyfuss was working with the Minneapolis-Honeywell Regulator Company in the creation of both consumer items like the Chronotherm and industrial components such as housings for gas valves and linkage covers. Honeywell was involved not solely with specific devices but also with systems. Industrial design had proven its

Minneapolis-Honeywell Regulator Co., logotype, c. 1937. The MH logo is contained within the modified rectangle that characterized both the outline of the Chronotherm thermostat (as shown) and Dreyfuss's later logo design of the Honeywell H. This formal device was used by Dreyfuss to create a sense of continuity in Honeywell's products in spite of the many changes that occurred over the years.

worth in addressing not just sales appeal, in the phraseology of the 1930s, but improved function. Questions of the role of appearance in design become more complicated when a mass audience and the desire to encourage mass consumption are also involved. A designer shaping a flagship locomotive does not face the same constraints as one working on a washing-machine design meant to appeal to an upper- and middle-class clientele (as was the case in Dreyfuss's work on the Sears, Roebuck & Co. Toperator and the higher priced version for Associated Merchandising Corporation, both produced by the Nineteen Hundred Corporation of Buffalo).[30] For Henry Dreyfuss, generating a sense of cohesiveness through all these categories of design, high and low, consumer and industrial, was a primary concern. If we observe the same formal elements being used over a range of categories by the same designer, it is not illogical to see these as a manifestation of his desire to create a sense of cohesiveness within a corporate appearance.[31]

Dreyfuss addressed sales appeal in the case of the Chronotherm by first redesigning the MH logo, making it more linear and uniform, while retaining the "survival form" of the serif on the M, and then relating it to the linear treatment of the Chronotherm casing. In this manner he was reiterating formal themes in a way that stressed the comprehensiveness of his approach, making it "all one thing," while creating a design with immediate visual interest. In the case of industrial components, Dreyfuss strove for a visual solidity of form, stressing mass and eliminating visible screws, which he combined with attention to color, graphics, and proportion. By the 1950s, the application of these concepts on an item-by-item basis had reached the level of giving a "family appearance" to Honeywell's products across all categories. In a now-lost rendering by Roland Stickney, dated May 29, 1950, a proposed round Chronotherm appears among both thermostats and industrial gauges. Dreyfuss's designers were soon generating guides to camber and radius treatments for box-type covers for industrial components, giving them a look of quality that did away with the sheet-metal aesthetic of the engineer.[32]

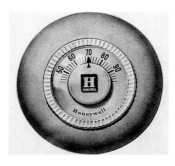

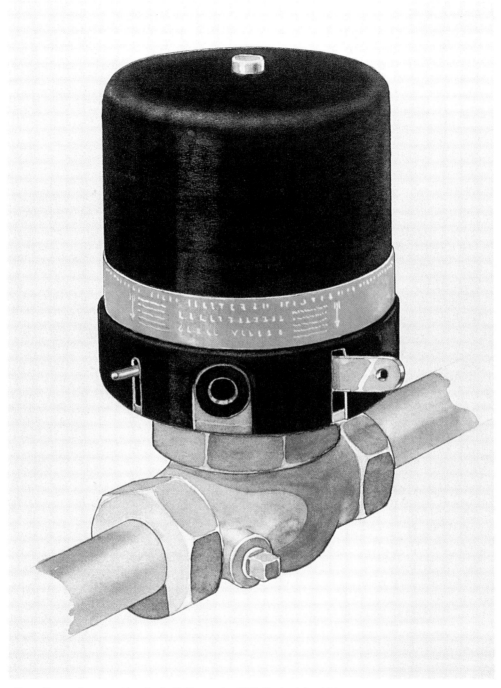

Above: Honeywell, proposed housing for V-15 gas valve, 1937. Dreyfuss's input into Honeywell's industrial line of products was being felt as early as the 1930s.

Left: Honeywell, T-86 thermostat, 1953. Detail from a Honeywell advertisement. The Round thermostat as it first appeared. Although a development program for this model was begun in 1940, further progress was delayed until after World War II and its associated priorities. Technology growing out of the war — clean room mercury switch manufacturing and bi-metal temperature sensors — contributed to the eventual success of the Honeywell Round.

Left: Sears, Roebuck & Co., Toperator washing machine, 1933.
Right: American Merchandising Corp., washing machine, 1933.
These two machines, both manufactured by the Nineteen Hundred Corporation
of Buffalo but sold through these two retailers, were mechanically quite
similar. The Toperator retained the speckled porcelain enamel finish of many
utilitarian items from the first quarter of the century, while the more "upscale"
AMC machine was available in a variety of colors, including a deep brown
with a goldtone horizontal band.

The genesis of the Round thermostat, arguably Dreyfuss's most enduring design, probably began in discussions between himself and the company president Harold W. Sweatt in 1940. H.W., as he was known, had been involved in the business since he was a teenager, having begun work under his father, W. R. Sweatt, and immediately following Mark Honeywell. He was keen on bringing Honeywell's marketing approach to a more sophisticated level to distinguish it from the competition. Dreyfuss's alter ego in the development of the Round was Carl Kronmiller, a design engineer who had come to Honeywell from Time-O-Stat Controls, a competitor purchased by Honeywell in 1931. According to Kronmiller's associate Carl Hoyt, another Honeywell employee, Kronmiller

> told me quite frankly that H.W. came to his area one day in 1940, sat down at his desk, and they talked about products. Carl told H.W., "We need a radically new thermostat. Why can't we make something a lot different from our competitors' models and different from our own thermostats?"
>
> Carl told me that as they talked, H.W. picked up a piece of paper and started drawing circles on it. Then he handed the paper to Carl and said, "Here. Go ahead and make something of it."[33]

This detail is especially telling as it also describes a working method that Dreyfuss used. In fact, one of his pastimes was attempting to draw perfect circles freehand. Proposals he drew for clients on cocktail napkins from the Plaza Hotel's Oak Room are numerous.[34] Dreyfuss also made the observation that rectangular thermostats (at this time, all thermostats were essentially rectangular or ovoid in shape) seemed to be impossible to mount on the wall without appearing crooked.[35] To further complicate the story of the Round, it should be noted that during Kronmiller's time as Time-O-Stat's design engineer, the company had manufactured a round thermostat of a sort prior to its absorption by Honeywell.[36]

Initial models of the Round thermostat differed considerably from the form we know today. From the front it appeared to be a solid, rounded disc of buff-colored metal or plastic, with the dominant element being a curved thermometer with a scale beneath it keyed to its rise and fall and to a central rotating disk that allowed the temperature to be raised or lowered. The earliest extant rendering of one of these models is dated April 1, 1942, which belies the accounts that say development ceased because of World War II. In fact, test models had been installed in Honeywell employees' homes a year prior to this date. A design patent for a "control instrument," this early version of the Round, was filed by Dreyfuss on June 19, 1942, and was granted design patent 136,850 on December 14, 1943. Carl Kronmiller filed for a patent on the mechanics of the same design on December 4, 1942, which was granted on February 12, 1946 (2,394,920). But Honeywell still did not have a functioning round thermostat it could market. However, two aspects of the final Honeywell Round first appeared in this line of development: a rendering from May 19, 1943, shows an "Acratherm w[ith] clear plastic cap[,] concentric line treatment wall plate." In the final version, the cap would be removable, allowing it to be painted to match the color of the room in which it was installed; the wall plate, considerably larger in diameter than the thermostat itself, would cover the outline of any previously installed thermostat that the Round replaced (it was designed from the start for "adjustable anticipation," as the company referred to it, meaning that it could substitute for any previously used thermostat).[37]

According to Honeywell, the program was revived in 1946. The chief problem with the existing format was the curved thermometer, which one source states had an 80 percent discard rate — only one in five functioned properly. Ultimately, it was done away with entirely, and the thermostat came to rely on a bimetallic coil thermometer (invisible with the cover in place) for sensing variations in room temperature. Methods developed during wartime production lowered the cost of manufacturing this item considerably and increased its reliability. Kronmiller and Dreyfuss introduced the concept of the plastic "picture window" to the thermostat's design. This called for considerable hand labor in painting half of the interior of the plastic dial, adding to the cost and slowing the production rate. The program abruptly came to a halt again in 1947, with the project now $58,000 in the red. Dated sketches by Dreyfuss and his staff, which are found on the firm's microfilm records, however, indicate that the office continued to work with per-

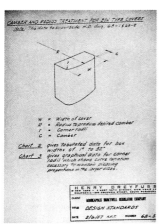

mutations of this idea. It was in 1948 that Dreyfuss seems to have first proposed a "Round Chronotherm," which would take the 1946 version of the design with the clear plastic window and add an electric clock. This was an updating of an idea he had worked with since his speculative proposals to Honeywell for thermostats in 1929. He would continue promoting this concept well into the early 1950s, when the Round reached its final form.

It was in early 1950 when a new marketing director at Honeywell saw considerable potential in the idea of a round thermostat. Herbert D. Bissell recalled that, despite Honeywell's domination of the market, he was stunned by how little their products differentiated themselves from those of their competitors. Further, he saw that the "plain-Jane" rectangular boxes being manufactured at that time as a major challenge in terms of creating an advertising campaign.[38] Apparently searching for any way out of the situation, Bissell recalled:

> One day I learned there was an old clay model of [a] round design gathering dust on a shelf in the engineering department. I went to see Charles B. Sweatt, brother of Harold and Executive V.P., and explaining our marketing dilemma, asked for permission to see what we could do with the round model. . . . The lead Heating Controls engineer was Carl Kronmiller. He welcomed my visit while claiming the round design was really his idea rather than that of Henry. . . .[39]

Honeywell, design standards for box-type covers for industrial components, drawn by Alvin Tilley, 1955. By the 1950s, standards had been developed for the appearance of the most mundane Honeywell products. An index of the effectiveness of industrial design is seen in such post-war creations where even engineered components have taken on the finish of consumer items.

Top: Deere & Co., John Deere Model R diesel tractor, 1949. The most powerful tractor to date in
the John Deere line, the Model R merited a new look befitting its strength. The vertical "meander"
radiator grill was Dreyfuss's idea, and gained him a design patent. It stemmed from his observation
that farmers needed to be able to rake debris from the machines using their gloved hands.

Bottom: Deere & Co., unstyled and styled Model A tractors. In this striking photograph, the marked
difference between the tractor's appearance before and after Dreyfuss's redesign is emphasized.

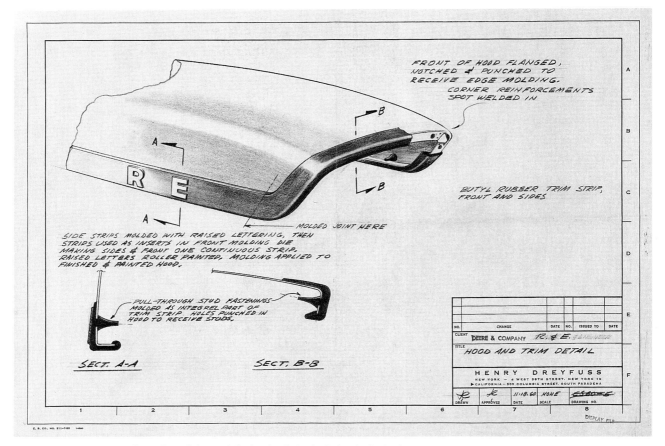

Above: Deere & Co., study for hood and trim detail, drawing by Jim Conner, 1959. This drawing gives us a glimpse into the thousands of drawings that went into the New Generation of Power's genesis. This, one of four left by Dreyfuss for this small detail alone, is indicative of the complexity of shaping a product that is both a work of engineering and a consumer item.

Right: Deere & Co., full-size clay study model of the hood for the proposed New Generation of Power tractor, c. 1958. The caption accompanying this publicity photograph reads: "This technique is used to determine a finished form when contours are critical." The generation of the final form turned out to be far more complex than this wood and clay model begins to suggest.

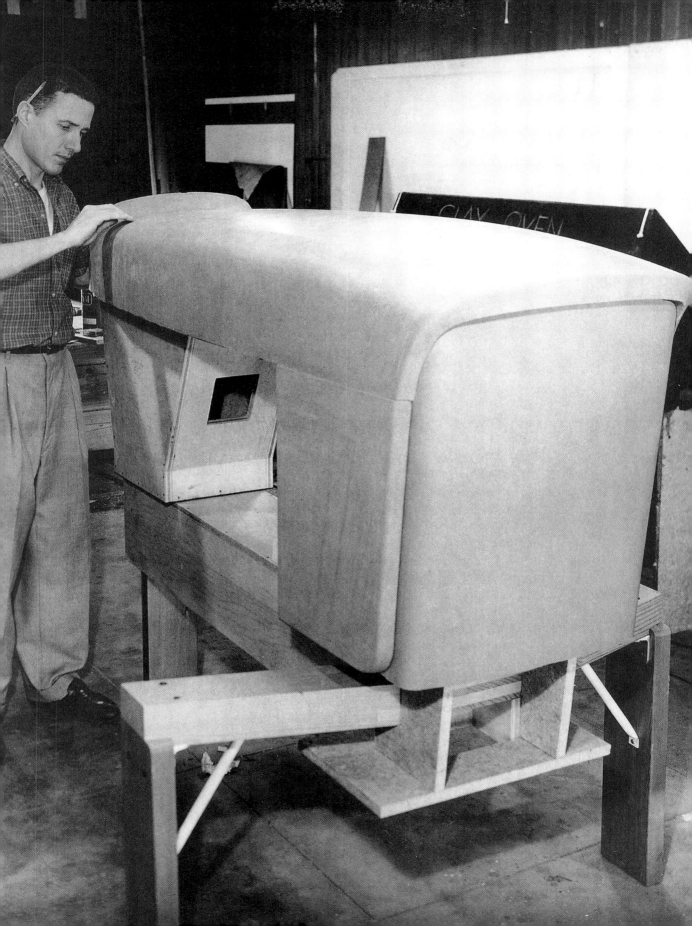

Deere & Co., cover of promotional brochure for new line of tractors, 1960. In this multi-page brochure we see the most striking aspect of the new tractor line: a subtly curved hood that was intended to look as if it was pulling even while at rest. The final appearance, a traditional green and yellow paint scheme that had identified John Deere tractors since 1924, was the outcome of hundreds of permutations.

they managed to create an image suited to its tremendous power. For the previous horizontal treatment of the radiator louvers, Dreyfuss substituted a vertical radiator grille, which was perforated for ventilation in a pattern that increased its surface area. This idea came from Dreyfuss's observation that farmers often had to rake chaff from the radiator grilles with their gloved hands, and the design (again, the recipient of a design patent) took this in to account.[53]

Deere & Co.'s tractors had been known for their robust character beginning with the Model D (1923), the first tractor to bear the name John Deere. Prior to 1960, all John Deere tractors were powered by two cylinders, mounted horizontally. This meant that individual engine components were relatively large, and their operators could serve as their own mechanics. Poppin' Johnnies, as the tractors became known because of the sound of their engines' exhaust, were served well by large, durable gears, a one-piece transmission case, and pressure lubrication to the main and connecting rod bearings and piston pins.[54] Demands for additional power, however, put an end to this format. At first the need was for operating attachments, hydraulics, and later for amenities such as air conditioning for enclosed cabs. To stay with the two-cylinder engine would have meant increasing the size of the pistons to such a degree that they could no longer be contained within a tractor of a size that could function between rows of crops.

Rather than simply accommodating the need for a redesigned engine, Deere & Co. management, in the persons of Charles Wiman, the chairman of the company during the inception of the program in 1955, and William Hewitt, his successor, opted for a complete redesign of the line of John Deere tractors.[55] For the first time, the nomenclature for referring to the various models would be standardized by numerical designations (there would be no more Model As, Bs, Rs, etc.). This meant that graphics for the tractors could also be unified. Field tests were done on the legibility of typefaces and colors at varying distances. Most important, perhaps, was the fact that a certain amount of redundancy and performance overlap between models could be eliminated through this complete revamping. Yet the program carried with it a large amount of risk: the buyers of agricultural equipment were known for their reluctance to embrace untried products. Since the U.S. companies producing tractors had, by this time, pooled many of their patents in a cooperative arrangement, the performance of similar machinery made by different firms often proved identical. It was understood that appearance would have to be a determining factor and that, in distinction to many industries, there would have to be a serious effort to create a reassuring continuity while introducing a radical change.

The most visible aspect of carryover from the previous equipment was the green-and-yellow paint scheme that had been a part of the aesthetic of John Deere tractors since the Model D. Yet even this was not ignored during the design phase: surviving sketches in the Dreyfuss Collection show the hoods of Deere & Co. tractors with

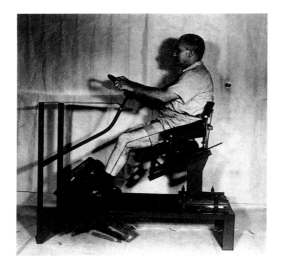
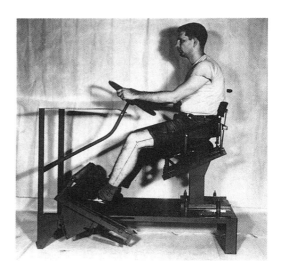
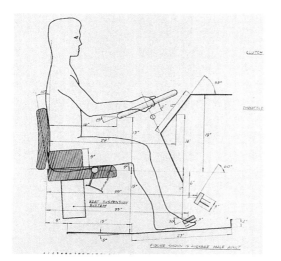
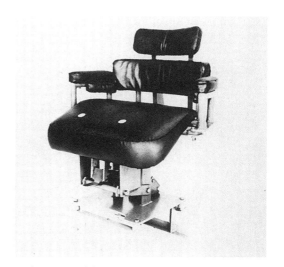

Deere & Co., report on new tractor seat, 1955. In this report we have a capsule summary of the Dreyfuss office's investigations into human comfort and safety. The first two images show short and tall operators seated in a mock-up of the new seat. An early Joe is shown in an analytical drawing by Alvin Tilley. Finally, we have an image of the first experimental seat executed in consultation with Dr. Janet Travell.

Deere & Co., tractor seat, designed 1960, this version 1965. In this image of the final seat design, shown here on a 4020 tractor, we see the levers that permit adjustment by the operator as well as the mechanism that allowed the seat to rise when the operator stood.

stainless steel panels, a number of predominantly yellow schemes, and even some suggestions that Dreyfuss's beloved brown was considered at one point by his designers. In
the end, the vibrant green punctuated by yellow detailing prevailed as it had in the past.
Dreyfuss's primary concern was with the overall impression created by the tractors'
hoods. Early in the planning stages he made the argument that the new tractors should
be able to accommodate liquid-propane storage tanks within their contours, rather than
being bolted onto the exterior as an apparent afterthought.[56] (The bulkiness of the fuel
versus that of kerosene or diesel caused this problem; its relative cheapness was the reason operators used it in the first place.) This concern was addressed by moving the fuel
tank to the front of the tractor, which increased operator safety to some degree but
made the tanks more liable to damage. Thus the tractors, viewed head-on, changed radically from their predecessors. Instead of the horizontal louvers of the tractors of the
'30s and '40s, or the vertical, "corrugated" radiator shields of the '40s and '50s, a solid
and substantial plate of painted steel now formed the "prow" (small vertical louvers
were added late in the design process to increase air flow to the engine compartment
for cooling). The radiator grille, so to speak, was now shifted to the sides of the tractor.
Two benefits accrued following this change: the addition of the heavier-gauge steel at
the front meant better support for the hood, which was to be a single, die-formed sheet
of steel, and for the industrial versions of the tractors which became front-loaders, no
additional protection needed to be added, substantially improving their appearance
over their predecessors. Dreyfuss had insisted from the early stages of the project that
the one-piece hood was feasible, citing the roofs of contemporary automobiles as proof.
Its curved form was to compensate for the varying dimensions of wheels that might be
outfitted on individual tractors. On most of the "New Generation" tractors, the one-
piece hood contributed to the visual impression that the vehicle was in the process of
pulling, reinforcing the notion that a new, more powerful engine was concealed underneath. As with most of his designs, Dreyfuss demanded in this case that visible seams,
screws, or anything that distracted from an impression of massiveness be avoided —
and that the joins in the metal panels be acknowledged.

The design of the seats for the new line of tractors was an undertaking of such
significance that it merits discussion. Even those unfamiliar with farm equipment
instantly recognize the steel seats, pressed into a saddle shape, that were first used in
the nineteenth century and were still the norm in the 1930s. One of Dreyfuss's earliest
proposals to Deere & Co. was for a seat that would have more comfortable slits rather
than the "cheeseholes" that served for ventilation and the drainage of rainwater if
equipment was left out in the elements. (Dreyfuss's proposal was rejected at the time
because all of the Deere & Co. divisions would have had to implement its use, and due
to the decentralized nature of the company, this was unlikely.) The design process at the
time prior to Dreyfuss's involvement with Deere was simplicity itself: the worker with

Deere & Co., 3010 tractor undergoing mud-bath test, 1960. Waterloo, Iowa, was
the locus for both the testing and production of the new Deere tractors. The
John Deere research and engineering center included this "obstacle course" for
the new machines.

the largest posterior dimensions was chosen as the model.[57] This changed markedly with the entrance of Dr. Janet Travell, who had been studying tractor operators from films provided to her by Dreyfuss. A specialist on muscular-skeletal disorders, she had contributed to earlier projects for Consolidated Vultee and was Dreyfuss's consultant of choice on seating. She apparently caused quite a stir when she appeared wearing green slacks and a yellow blouse for her first meeting with Deere's engineers, and probably some amusement when she took the driver's seat herself and piloted a tractor "at a snail's pace." She later wrote, "for awhile theory and practice seemed far apart," but she was gratified when the final design approached her initial conception quite closely.

> I was proud of the end product of my happy collaboration with Deere and Company's research and development team and with Henry Dreyfuss and his associates. When our seat was finally unveiled on a new line of John Deere tractors at the introductory show in Dallas, Texas, on August 30, 1960, I was told that one demonstration used a lanky tall Texan and a short fat boy to emphasize the quick adjustability of the tractor seat to accommodate operators comfortably.

> In that period of time, I was meeting with Presidential candidate John F. Kennedy in New York. From the start of the tractor seat project in January, 1953, I had stipulated that my name not be used in connection with any advertising, and my wishes were meticulously respected. I was a dark horse in tractor seat design.[58]

The seat was the ideal complement to the visual refinements made to the tractor. By mounting the moving, three-piece seat on a metal support angled at roughly twenty-seven degrees, a wide range of body types were accommodated. The seat slid down and forward to adapt to shorter operators; when a quick-release lever was pulled, the seat rose with the operator when he stood. An ingenious mechanism "remembered" the previous setting of the seat when the operator sat down again. This was very desirable, for farmers were in the habit of standing while driving tractors for a better view of their path and to stretch tired muscles during hours spent at the wheel. The bottom of the seat was inclined slightly forward to encourage operators to brace themselves with their leg muscles while moving over rough terrain; a lumbar support cushion for the lower back was extended to provide arms. The spring-mounted upper cushion allowed the driver to lean back and relax when riding on smooth terrain. Suspended by "rubber in torsion," the seat absorbed much of the shock that had plagued farmers since the introduction of mechanized agriculture.[59]

Prior to "Deere Day in Dallas," 136 tractors and 324 other pieces of machinery were shipped in relative secrecy to the location near the Cotton Bowl stadium where the events would be held in the gigantic parking lot. A more intimate introduction of the tractor, however, took place at the Neiman Marcus department store, where a gigantic gift box, complete with bow, appeared near the jewelry counter with a card telling customers they would soon see something that they had never seen in the store before

Deere & Co., 4010 row crop tractor, pulling five bottom plow, 1960. It is important to note that tractors did not operate in isolation but pulled various pieces
of equipment. These items were also designed by the Dreyfuss firm in conjunction with Deere's engineers. Here a publicity photograph from the new line's
debut year gives an indication of their striking appearance.

when the box was opened. On hand that day were Bill Hewitt; Tish Hewitt who, presented with shears on a velvet cushion, cut the bow; Stanley Marcus, the presiding marketing genius of the store; and his friend Henry Dreyfuss. When the sides of the massive package were lowered, the assembled crowd beheld a brand-new John Deere tractor, decorated with a number of diamond accessories that Marcus had attached to it at such key points as the exhaust stack. A model in pearlescent sequined coveralls stood astride the green-and-yellow machine. A few weeks later a chanteuse named Marlene Dietrich bought the coveralls.[60] A distinctly American cultural milestone was reached that day. Henry Dreyfuss, clad in brown, was in his element.

NOTES

1. Dreyfuss was president of the Society of Industrial Designers in 1947 and of the newly united Industrial Designers Society of America in 1965. The latter unified the Society of Industrial Designers (renamed the American Society of Industrial Designers in 1955) with the Industrial Designers Institute (founded as the American Designers Institute in 1938) and the Industrial Designers Education Association.

2. "The Role of the Industrial Designer," *Product Engineering* (September 1950) (clipping in Dreyfuss Collection).

3. Gilbert Seldes, foreword to Henry Dreyfuss, *A Record of Industrial Designs, 1929 through 1947* (New York: Davis, Delaney, 1947), 2.

4. William F. H. Purcell, interview with author, March 16–17, 1991.

5. Niels Diffrient, interview with author, March 1, 1991.

6. Henry Dreyfuss, "Industrial Design: Profile of an Organization," 3, transcript of a speech delivered before General George Doriots's class in manufacturing, Harvard University Graduate School of Business Administration, Cambridge, Massachusetts, November 9, 1965, Dreyfuss Collection.

7. For his time against these retainers, Dreyfuss initially charged $75 to $100 per hour (later, in the 1950s, $150 per hour). Rita Hart, interview by author, April 22, 1996. These amounts, among the highest charged by anyone in the profession, were greeted with disbelief by his contemporaries. Dreyfuss also insisted on yearly contracts with clients that retained him "to make sure you still love us" (i.e., the Dreyfuss firm). This is confirmed by copies of the contracts in the Deere & Co. Archives in East Moline, Illinois.

8. For an example of Everett's proficiency, see the article he coauthored with Robert H. Hose, "The Mechanics of Industrial Design," *Product Engineering* 24 (January 1, 1953), 121–28.

9. Donald M. Genaro, interview with author, October 16, 1990.

10. Henry Dreyfuss et al., "Norman Bel Geddes (1893–1958)," *Industrial Design* 5 (June 1958), 51.

11. "Henry Dreyfuss: Man in a Hurry" [U.S. Steel advertisement], *Industrial Design* 7 (October 1960), 19–21.

12. Unfortunately, Julian G. Everett and Robert H. Hose, Dreyfuss's partners in New York during the 1950s, left behind few written documents about their years with Dreyfuss other than published works.

13. Robert H. Fetridge, "Along the Highways and Byways of Finance," *New York Times*, June 18, 1950, financial section.

14. According to industrial designer Don Wallance, there were thirty staff members at the time of the creation of the Model 500 telephone; see *Shaping America's Products* (New York: Reinhold Publishing Company, 1956), 43. In 1958, the Dreyfuss office was reorganized after an extensive look into problems with the chain of command in the day-to-day management of client accounts. A partnership, which had begun in 1930 with Dreyfuss, Marks, and Hart, and which by 1952 had come to include Everett, Hose, and Purcell, was dissolved; only Purcell remained as a partner. Heads of accounts were now referred to as associates. In effect, Everett and Hose had been demoted. The situation was especially difficult in light of the fact that Hose and Purcell were brothers-in-law. Everett retired within a few years, and Hose opened his own office, where he was followed by several Dreyfuss accounts, Hoover being among them. Hose was president of the Society of Industrial Designers from 1953 to 1954.

15. *Rita Hart.* Occasionally you would have think tank sessions, he would call them that. *Don Genaro.* Henry would oftentimes pull in people that had no experience within a given area in an effort to try to show up some fresh ideas. Industrial designers pride themselves on being able to switch gears very quickly. *Rita Hart.* The outside point of view. *Don Genaro.* The outside point of view, exactly. And sometimes he would bring people in who were not working on telephones or tractors or whatever, and stir them up. And it paid off. Rita Hart and Don Genaro, interview with author, February 5, 1991. "Dreyfuss would throw out a hundred ideas. Maybe ninety-seven of them were no good, but three of them would be the best. And Henry insisted that you couldn't get those three without the other ninety-seven." Donald Holden, interview with author, February 20, 1991.

16. Niels Diffrient, interview with author, March 1, 1991.

17. Jim Conner related the following story: He had been working with Bill Purcell (who had been heading a particular project for Deere & Co. along with many others) for about a week on a roll assembly, similar to a roll bar used in dune buggies and other open vehicles. Working in the South Pasadena office one Saturday, Conner was approached by Dreyfuss who asked him what he was working on. Conner showed him a series of drawings that Dreyfuss felt looked too irregular or skewed for the kind of solid image he wanted to convey. When Conner replied that he thought he should talk to Purcell about the matter, "Dreyfuss went red just like a cartoon character." It was clear that he was furious with even the suggestion that he was not exercising ultimate control in this case. No harsh words were exchanged, and Dreyfuss returned to apologize some fifteen minutes later. But Conner felt that this instance was as close as he had come to ending his career with the organization. Jim Conner, interview with author, October 16, 1990.

18. Ibid.

19. J. A. Odom, senior principal, Industrial Design Department, Residential/Business Controls, Honeywell, Golden Valley, Minnesota, letter to author, February 27, 1996.

20. These were published as *Industrial Design: A Pictorial Accounting* in the years mentioned and as *Industrial Design: Volume 5* at some unspecified date between 1960 and 1968.

21. Dreyfuss habitually dressed in brown from the early 1930s. Gilbert Seldes mentioned this point in a biographical sketch published in the *The New Yorker*. This penchant arose partly from the practical concern of having his clothing match when he traveled. However, the fact that Dreyfuss owned a set of evening clothes in brown leads one to believe that this eccentricity allowed him to set himself off from the blue- and gray-suited executives he constantly rubbed elbows with. Seldes, "Profiles: Artist in a Factory," *The New Yorker* 7 (August 29, 1931), 22–24.

22. Herbert D. Bissell, former corporate vice president of marketing, Honeywell, Minneapolis, letter to author, August 26, 1993. Bissell was director of merchandising for Honeywell at the time under discussion.

23. Bill Purcell, interview with author, March 16–17, 1991.

24. John Dreyfuss and Gail Dreyfuss Wilson, interview with author, November 23, 1990.

25. Mildred Constantine, interview with author, February 26, 1991.

26. George Nelson, in "Henry Dreyfuss 1904–1972," *Industrial Design* 20 (March 1973), 42–43. For an initial assessment of Nelson's own practical and theoretical approach to design, see Stanley Abercrombie, *George Nelson: The Design of Modern Design* (Cambridge, Mass.: MIT Press, 1995).

27. Dreyfuss, "Does America Have a Design Heritage?" *Product Engineering* (May 18, 1959) (clipping in Dreyfuss Collection).

28. Terence Riley and Edward Eigen, "Between the Museum and the Marketplace: Selling Good Design," *Studies in Modern Art* 4 (1994), 161. Riley and Eigen make this comparison in pointing out the "elasticity" of Edgar Kaufmann, Jr.'s "definition of reasonable cost" in the choices for the "Good Design" exhibitions.

29. Honeywell Inc., the Minneapolis-Honeywell Regulator Company at this time, was later successful in trademarking both the word "Round"(trademark number 1,439,016, granted May 12, 1987) and the shape itself (Trade Mark 1622108, granted November 13, 1990). (This information courtesy Clyde Blinn and Fred Lange, retired Honeywell patent attorneys, and conveyed to the author by Herbert Bissell in a letter dated August 26, 1993.) The thermostat was properly known at the time of its introduction on October 15, 1953, as the T86 (Honeywell *Circulator* [house organ] 17 (October 15, 1953), 1). A "Golden Jubilee Round" with a larger central dial was introduced in 1960 to coincide with the company's seventy-fifth anniversary. Modified again in 1964 to accommodate central air conditioning — and known as the T87 — this is the version most commonly seen today.

30. See design patents for "Combined Wringer and Casing for a Washing Machine" 89,879 (May 16, 1933) and "Combined Wringer and Casing for a Washing Machine" 90,616 (September 5, 1933).

31. It can be argued that Peter Behrens, in his work for the Allgemeine Elektrizitäts Gesellschaft during the first decade of the twentieth century, defined both corporate identity and the role of the industrial designer. See Stanford Anderson, "Modern Architecture and Industry: Peter Behrens, the AEG, and Industrial Design," *Oppositions* 21 (Summer 1980), 78–97; Tilmann Buddensieg and Henning Rogge, *Industriekultur: Peter Behrens und die AEG, 1907–1914* (Berlin: Mann, 1979), translated into English as *Peter Behrens and the AEG* (Cambridge, Mass.: MIT Press, 1984); Hans-Joachim Kadatz, *Peter Behrens: Architeckt — Maler — Grafiker — und Formgestalter, 1868–1940* (Leipzig: E. A. Seeman Verlag, 1977); and Alan Windsor, *Peter Behrens: Architect and Designer* (New York: Whitney Library of Design, 1981).

32. The "design standards," as they are labeled, are dated March 24, 1954 (project 68-2), and appear in a notebook titled "Status of Design Projects 11/1/53 – 9/1/54" found in the Client Response Files in the Dreyfuss Collection. Similarly, when the Honeywell logotype was redesigned by Dreyfuss in 1951, a fifteen-page bible of its proper usage in company designs, publications, and advertisements was also published. For the introduction of the new logo, see Honeywell *Circulator* [house organ] for Friday, October 26, 1951, 3. The new logo echoed the shape of the 1938 Chronotherm.

33. "Thermostat Still Moves Round the World After 30 Years," *Honeywell World* (Centennial issue), January 7, 1985, 13.

34. Even "informal" proposals were studied well in advance, and Dreyfuss's decision regarding when to make his pitch and the tools he would utilize at that time came from his on-the-spot personal reading of the client. Don Genaro, interview with author, October 16, 1990.

35. "Architectural Products by Industrial Designers," *Progressive Architecture* (June 1964), 15.

36. The Time-O-Stat thermostat had a vertical thermometer attached to its face, and it used a mercury switch as well as a coiled bimetallic strip — the last two features appeared in the final version of the Round.

37. "Thermostat Still Moves Round the World After 30 Years," 13.

38. "I came to Honeywell from a Toledo company where I directed a large advertising program involving magazines and radio and television networks. I tell you this because coming to Honeywell proved to a be major shock. The problem: I found there was nothing to promote to consumers other than the current wall thermostat. It was a plain-Jane rectangular box with no distinctiveness from the competition. It was tough, if not impossible, to merchandise." Herbert D. Bissell, letter to author, August 26, 1993. "I can only tell you what I found when I arrived and essentially [I] had nothing to promote in the box-like product on the wall of millions of American homes. . . ." Herbert D. Bissell, Minneapolis, letter to Amy Chen, Stern School of Business, New York University, July 5, 1994.

39. Bissell, letter to author, August 26, 1993.

40. Contaminants such as dust caused the mercury to separate in the thermometers and created short-circuits in the switches.

41. Bissell, letter to Amy Chen, July 5, 1994.

42. "Thermostat Still Moves Round the World After 30 Years," 13.

43. Honeywell *Circulator* [house organ], November 26, 1953, 3.

44. The advertisement appeared in the *Saturday Evening Post* for October 31, 1953; *Life* magazine for November 9, 1953; and the November issues of *American Home* and *Better Homes and Gardens*. Dreyfuss had consulted with Honeywell and its divisions on a total of twenty-nine projects between November 1, 1953, and August 1, 1954, according to the "Status of Design Projects" notebook in the Dreyfuss Collection.

45. Dreyfuss, "Adapting Products to People," *Bell Telephone Magazine* 46 (September/October 1967), 23, also quoted in the *Wall Street Journal*, January 8, 1968, "Notable and Quotable," editorial page.

46. Dreyfuss, "The Car Detroit Should Be Building," *Consumer Reports* 23 (July 1958), 351–55. Emphasis in original. Dreyfuss was of course not alone in his criticism; even Raymond Loewy, as implicated in styling as any designer of his age, managed to cast brickbats at Detroit while waiting for Studebaker's last gasp in South Bend, Indiana. That last gasp turned out to be Loewy's Avanti of 1962. Earl, head of styling for General Motors since the 1930s, left GM in 1959 and established an industrial design firm under his own name.

47. Dreyfuss, speech to the Thirteenth Annual Conference, Reinforced Plastics Division, Society of the Plastics Industry, February 6, 1958, quoted in "Clips and Quotes," *Industrial Design* 5 (May/June 1958), 8. Emphasis in original.

48. Frank Walters, Product Engineering, John Deere Waterloo Tractor Works, to H. D. Witzel, director, Product Planning, Deere & Co., February 5, 1975, File #19014, Deere & Co. Archives. Witzel adds in a note to the executive office to which this letter was attached that "Following this visit in early 1937, the Industrial Design work was started on the Model 'B' resulting in Waterloo Work Order 6923-G of September 27, 1937 . . . ," making this the first assignment Dreyfuss undertook for Deere & Co.

49. The early design work on the Model B and Model A tractors by Dreyfuss and Barnhart is documented in File 2330, Deere & Co. Archives, East Moline, Illinois. Progress Report #2 of November 24, 1937, details the changes recommended to Deere & Co.

50. Design patent 112,365 (November 29, 1938).

51. Bill Davidson, "You Buy Their Dreams," *Collier's* 120 (August 2, 1947), 23.

52. For additional background on Deere & Co. tractors, see Wayne G. Broehl, Jr., *John Deere's Company* (New York: Doubleday & Company, 1984); Randy Leffingwell, *John Deere Farm Tractors: A History of the John Deere Tractor* (Osceola, Wis.: Motorbooks International, 1993); Will McCracken, *John Deere Tractors, 1918–1976* (Lincoln, Neb.: Deere & Co., 1976); and Robert C. Williams, *Fordson, Farmall, and Poppin' Johnny: A History of the Farm Tractor and Its Impact on America* (Urbana and Chicago: University of Illinois Press, 1987).

53. Strother MacMinn, interview with author, November 24, 1990.

54. McCracken, *John Deere Tractors*, 6.

55. Wiman died soon after the inception of the program. William Alexander Hewitt had mar-

ried Wiman's daughter, Patricia ("Tish") Deere Wiman, in 1948 and, soon after joining Deere & Co., had risen through the ranks of the sales force, beginning in his native San Francisco with the John Deere Plow Company. His familiarity with Europe from his work there following World War II, his education at Harvard Business School and the connections resulting therefrom, and his personal interest in matters of art and design took the company to a new level of sophistication. This was most visible in its headquarters building in Moline, Illinois, begun by Eero Saarinen (his final project) and completed by his partner Kevin Roche. Dreyfuss, along with Robert McNamara, was a fundamental influence on Hewitt's choice of Saarinen as architect for the project. See Broehl, *John Deere's Company*, 635–38.

56. William F. H. Purcell, "Industrial Design, A Vital Ingredient: A Study of Its Application to the New John Deere Tractors," *Automotive Industries*, May 15, 1961, unpaginated offprint in Publicity Files, Dreyfuss Collection.

57. Hewitt recalled one old hand at Deere & Co. describing the process as follows:

"I remember when we would get old Pete, who had the biggest ass, and sit him in plaster of Paris." William Hewitt, telephone interview with author, March 14, 1991.

58. Janet Travell, *Office Hours: Day and Night* (New York: World Publishing Co., 1968), 286 ff. Travell went on to become both Kennedy's and Lyndon Johnson's personal physician during their respective terms as president.

59. Purcell, "Industrial Design, A Vital Ingredient."

60. Bill Hewitt, telephone interview with author, October 10, 1995.

Chapter 5: THE 1960s

THE LIMITS OF DESIGN

We bear in mind that the object being worked on is going to be ridden in, sat upon, looked at, talked into, activated, operated or in some other way used by people.

When the point of contact between the product and the people becomes a point of friction, then the industrial designer has failed.

On the other hand, if people are made safer, more efficient, more comfortable — or just plain happier — by contact with the product, then the designer has succeeded.[1]

WHEN HENRY DREYFUSS REVISED HIS CREDO between 1957 and some time in the mid-1960s, he removed a key phrase from the third paragraph, where he had stated that the industrial designer had succeeded if he made people more eager to purchase.[2] What had changed in his attitude toward design that distanced him from his earlier stance? In 1953 he told the American Association of Advertising Agencies:

It is indisputable that a measure of the value of both our services is sales. If we designers don't come up with a product that has sales appeal, then we have failed our client.[3]

Twelve years later, Dreyfuss stood as spokesman for the profession, and such candor regarding consumer appeal seemed unbecoming to the president of the Industrial Designers Society of America. By gathering all of the industrial-design-oriented professional organizations under one roof (the newly created IDSA), there was to be a new, unified voice for all designers. This was a very different vision from that of the founders of the Society of Industrial Designers in 1944, where the exclusivity of the club was ensured by requiring that members show evidence of having produced designs in three different areas (in other words, those who designed only automobiles or anything else within a single category of design were not eligible for membership). Having a long-standing interest in educational issues relating to design, Dreyfuss

Polaroid Corp., Automatic 100 Land Camera, 1963. This breakthrough camera introduced Polaroid photography to the broadest audience it had yet enjoyed. The weight of the camera was 50 percent less than its predecessors, and it could take either color or black-and-white photographs.

seems to have been chosen for the presidency by consensus. In his statement to the new society, Dreyfuss wrote, "In any age, but particularly in the mid-20th Century, to stand still is to slip backward. And of course this is what the profession of industrial designers is dedicated to — to take what is good today and make it better for more people tomorrow, because making anything better is the only road to human happiness."[4] The confidence reflected in this statement was part of the ethic of his generation, and of course particularly important to Dreyfuss in light of his personal background.

A shift in sensibility, however, was brewing in the late 1960s and 1970s. The editor of *Industrial Design* magazine for many years, Ralph Caplan, who knew the cast of characters well, found the ranking of the first generation of industrial designers academic:

Henry Dreyfuss was sometimes called "the dean of American industrial designers." Walter Dorwin Teague, a contemporary of Dreyfuss, was also called that. I don't know why industrial design should have two deans — I don't even know why it should have one — but of the two, Dreyfuss was more deanlike: mellow, eminently successful, warm and accessible to colleagues, although less intellectual in style than Teague. Maybe Teague was Dean of Academic Affairs and Dreyfuss was Dean of Students.[5]

Caplan's claim of not knowing why there should be a "dean" of design was to question the very system that Teague, Dreyfuss, and others had hoped to establish with the creation of the SID.[6] Leadership was the critical issue to the first generation, and seniority was part of the equation. Niels Diffrient, the man Dreyfuss groomed to replace him in the role he had created for himself, reveals the ambivalence toward authority that characterized this next generation:

. . . by the time I got there [to the Dreyfuss office in 1955] the philosophy of avoiding styling was quite entrenched. Actually, too much so, to the degree that Henry had gotten the reputation of being the "gray designer." And that was a term that went around . . . a lot of people criticized our conservative approach, even within the office, myself for one. Because a lot of the stuff was too conservative, it didn't take advantage of the potential to put some life into it. I would guess that was probably at the bottom of my discontent there, that we didn't really struggle hard enough to go beyond just solving the problem, and give the thing some real life or excellence beyond the expected. The forms were never really surprising; they were always good and solid, honest, straightforward, useful, all of that. But often we didn't take the extra step, I felt. Of course some things came out remarkably well, I have to admit. But that's the reason that it lasted.[7]

Diffrient, who worked for Dreyfuss in California, was invited to have a drink with Doris and Henry one evening after work. Not merely a social gesture, Dreyfuss was aware that

Henry Dreyfuss with Niels Diffrient, 1966. In a publicity photograph taken in 1966, Dreyfuss confers with Diffrient, an associate in his firm, during work on the Edison Electric Institute-sponsored transmission tower project. Diffrient was groomed by Dreyfuss to assume his role as the profession's conscience. In the 1970s and the 1980s, Diffrient's prominence in the profession bore out Dreyfuss's faith in him.

Diffrient was feeling some frustration with the operating procedures long established in the office; the younger man understood that this husband-and-wife team were trying to figure him out.

> I still remember he and Doris sitting with me, saying, "Well, just what is it you want?" I can still remember the looks on their faces. It came through to me, at that moment, that they must have been somewhat dumbfounded, as to what was troubling me. Then I realized I didn't know what I wanted.[8]

In this Diffrient had much in common with many Americans in the 1960s, but not with Dreyfuss and Marks. Brought up within a system of beliefs that stressed duty to one's fellow man and "dedicated to the ever increasing knowledge and practice and love of the right,"[9] it must have seemed inconceivable to them that someone of Diffrient's intelligence and ability would not follow their path. Their friend Connie Constantine understood their orientation and the bond it forged between them:

> No evaluation [of Dreyfuss] would be complete without the mention of Doris Marks Dreyfuss, his wife, as many of his accomplishments belong to both of them.... Mrs. Dreyfuss' contribution was her insistence upon absolute clarity of meaning with simplicity of expression.[10]

While Connie Constantine spoke specifically of the Dreyfusses' last great project, the *Symbol Sourcebook*,[11] her apt phrasing of Doris Marks's aesthetic permits a glimpse into the role Marks played beyond the business side of the firm. The linkage between appearance and legitimacy became increasingly important to the Dreyfusses during the same period that most industrial designers were catering to consumer tastes in a manner that some have characterized as craven. Henry Dreyfuss, the firm, was to be above "styling," and yet it had its origins within that very approach.

A rationale for this aversion to styling is implied in Terrence Riley's and Edward Eigen's critique of the Good Design exhibitions planned by the Museum of Modern Art in the 1950s under the direction of Edgar Kaufmann, Jr. While acknowledging the importance of the generation born prior to the twentieth century, they stated that:

> the majority of those whose talents were featured in Good Design were born in the first two decades of the twentieth century ... [and] primarily completed their education and apprenticeships after the Paris Exposition Internationale des Arts Décoratifs et Industriels Modernes in 1925 and before the outbreak of World War II in 1939. They had in common the experience of spending their early careers designing for societies conditioned by the privations of economic depression and wartime.

Of the designers listed by the authors, Dreyfuss is clearly the most industrially (mass production) oriented.[12] Creating an imagery of plenty in the midst of "the privations of economic depression and wartime" was a tall order, and the intelligent mediation between luxury and utility is undoubtedly one of the strongest attributes of Dreyfuss's body of work. The designs were restrained, but the restraints were largely his own, in a

Henry Dreyfuss at a 1972 exhibition of materials for *Symbol Sourcebook: An Authoritative Guide to International Graphic Symbols*. The book, assembled by Dreyfuss, Doris Marks, and assistant Paul Clifton, was an outgrowth of work begun in the 1950s. It was aimed at alleviating the difficulties of labeling products in the languages of all the nations where they were sold. This comprehensive guide showed the Dreyfusses' particular skills in gathering, evaluating, and presenting information.

self-imposed system that sought to put useful, attractive designs before the public in a commercial environment. In addition, Dreyfuss is almost without exception presented to readers as the youngest of the first generation of industrial designers, and, under Riley and Eigen's conception, he is viewed as part of the mainstream, not as a junior member.[13] Dreyfuss was suspicious of the attitudes toward industrial design found at the Museum of Modern Art. Visited by a delegation from the museum to discuss the possibility of a one-man show, he placed his office's output on display through sketches and models. One member of the group remarked,

> "The numerals on this clock dial seem out of proportion." Another asked, "Why did you put that chrome on the bottom of the typewriter?" Rather than try to explain, I suggested that we forget the idea of an exhibit. It occurred to me that the only museums in which I care to show my work are places like Macy's, Marshall Field's, and the May Company, and I hope never to have a permanent exhibit in any of them.[14]

Dreyfuss's disdain for both grandstanding and the aesthetic niceties of the fine arts establishment masked his feelings about having to compromise his own taste at times to retain clients.

Having been shaped by the Depression and World War II, he had developed a design philosophy conditioned by adversity. A master of the soft sell, he found himself cast with increasing frequency in the role of salesman, while others took care of the messy details of design. Part of his success came from the selection of talent he had assembled in the two previous decades: Bill Purcell, his sole partner after 1958, would, with Jim Conner, Niels Diffrient, and Don Genaro, become Henry Dreyfuss Associates in 1969. By the end of the 1950s, all four men were working with him. Purcell, Conner, and Diffrient lived in California as Dreyfuss did. As they proved their competency, the day-to-day design aspects for major clients became their provinces. Purcell worked with Deere & Co. engineers while Dreyfuss discussed color schemes with its chairman, Bill Hewitt. Conner likewise consulted with Polaroid Corporation's engineers and production managers on the SX-70 camera while Dreyfuss presented leather samples for the same to Edwin Land, founder of Polaroid. Dreyfuss was being replaced as a designer by men with specific talents he lacked (in engineering or architecture) or by those educated specifically in design. One of the latter was Charles Pelly, educated at Pasadena's Art Center College of Design and the Konstfackskolan, the Swedish National College of Art, Craft, and Design in Stockholm. After a brief stint with the design firm Latham Tyler Jensen, Pelly was hired by

Top: Founding partners of Henry Dreyfuss Associates from left to right: James Conner, Donald M. Genaro, Niels Diffrient, and William F. H. Purcell. Upon Henry Dreyfuss's retirement, effective January 1, 1969, Purcell, Conner, Genaro, and Diffrient formed Henry Dreyfuss Associates.

Bottom: Rita Hart joined Henry Dreyfuss as the firm's office manager in 1930. Until the Dreyfusses left the organization in 1969, Miss Hart was the best interpreter of their unspoken priorities to other members of the office. Probably the closest to the Dreyfusses of any of their employees, she was their partner as well until the reorganization of the firm in 1958.

Edison Electric Institute, Double Y, Steel Tangent Tower, 230 kv Class, Double
Circuit, 1968. In one of his final industrial design projects, Dreyfuss attempted
to mediate between opposing forces: power companies that needed to transmit
ever larger amounts of electricity over greater distances and a budding environmental movement that saw the transmission lines and their towers as an
aesthetic imposition on the landscape.

Edison Electric Institute, Wood Pole Design, Tangent Tower, 230 kv Class, Single Circuit Model, 1968. Working with partner Bill Purcell and associate Niels Diffrient, Dreyfuss confronted the inherent divide between aesthetics and engineering in the EEI "power tower" project. Basically they sought honesty in form and an appropriate use of materials. A series of photographs of scale models such as this one helped make their case persuasive.

Dreyfuss in 1962 as a "grunt," as he put it. His was "sort of a love/hate relationship" with Dreyfuss, which stemmed from his admiration for Dreyfuss's practical way of handling his clients (and trying to make profits for them) coupled with some contempt for "all that old classic stuff" and the egotism typical of the first-generation industrial designers. In what might be described as a cynical, or simply realistic, assessment of the job, Pelly says that Dreyfuss once stated "designers are here to make the rich richer."[15] It is interesting to note that Pelly felt there were few "Art Center types" (i.e., from the fine arts side of the spectrum of design schools) in the California office. Among the ones who stayed the longest were himself, Conner, and Diffrient; the last two were graduates of Cranbrook Academy of Art in the 1950s. Along with Pratt Institute graduate Don Genaro, this was "the next generation."

Dreyfuss still took tremendous interest in certain projects. He and Diffrient began working on a major presentation to the Edison Electric Institute (EEI) in the wake of the first public outcries against high-voltage electrical transmission towers (for aesthetic reasons more than for health concerns at the time). As Dreyfuss was involved with the South Pasadena Beautiful and Los Angeles Beautiful organizations on his own time, his concern was two-fold: personally he sided with the "aesthetes" who wanted the power lines buried, but he was sympathetic to the utility companies who knew that the cost would be astronomical.[16] It was in fact the sort of challenge for which Dreyfuss was uniquely suited: to make the necessary invisible, and when visible, attractive. He had ample experience in dealing with domestic items like telephones and thermostats, but concealing a "power tower" in the midst of a path of clear-cut landscape was a challenge on a different scale entirely. The EEI had charged the Task Force on Environment, on which Dreyfuss sat as the principal figure regarding aesthetics, with developing "universally acceptable" designs.

As one might have expected, considering Dreyfuss's orientation toward robustness and seamlessness, the forms generated tended to be sturdy and unified-looking in contrast to their spindly predecessors; they made the combination of materials (steel, wood, aluminum, fiberglass-reinforced plastic, concrete) a virtue in generating a variety of appearances. Dreyfuss and Diffrient justified this by considering the task each category of tower had to perform and seeking an appropriate and "functional" appearance for it. Here again was the theoretical dilemma of modern design: where does function end if part of the function of a design is to have universal appeal? Dreyfuss and Diffrient were exploring the limits of design, effectively questioning what an object is, and how it differs from architecture. When does a product become a public work or resource? What does the public expect beyond the mere solving of problems on an engineering level? One aphorism regarding the utilitarian approach of the engineer is that "an engineer can do for one dollar what any fool can do for two." The latticed (open trusswork) steel predecessors of the Dreyfuss-designed towers

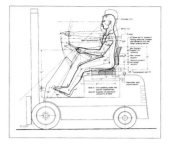

functioned perfectly well for carrying power lines and holding down costs, but something more was needed. Deciding what that "something more" should be and how it should be constituted was Henry Dreyfuss's area of expertise. He sold himself on a track record of basic designs for a consumer market and implied that this experience was applicable to the design of transmission towers. Dreyfuss was expected to know what would satisfy "the people" — or at least those people who were politically active. He found himself cast in the role of a modern-day Everyman, in which his personal tastes were, in effect, to substitute for opinion polls.

In contrast to the design of the transmission towers, much of Dreyfuss's work depended on the role of anthropometry. It is important to note that this role was more subtle and complicated in the actual creation of designs by the Dreyfuss firm than some have implied.[17] The charts of Joe and Josephine, the "typical" Americans devised by the Dreyfuss firm during the 1950s, did not, in fact, create a "universal yardstick" for the generation of all designs for human use, nor did they claim to. They were guidelines for designers to use in preliminary investigations; consideration of the specifics of any given situation relied on the individual designer's insights into human behavior. Certain aspects of human factors were restricted to the most basic perceptions: for example, that color can be distinguished only within a segment of the total zone of vision (i.e., most people can discern shapes over a broader range than they can color). Yet the objectivity that these charts provided in approaching new challenges was helpful, and they gave Dreyfuss a resource that was not available to the profession at large until he published *The Measure of Man* in 1960. The charts also provided him with an additional sales tool. Who could disagree with the layout of a new design that incorporated the needs of what appeared to be the "universal man"? In short, the new approach had the appearance of taking the "guesswork" out of the design process. The "scientific" aura of this strategy must have impressed many potential clients.

It is illuminating to note that the Dreyfuss office was aware of the nature of the compromise that was behind the human factors charts. In an interoffice memo of December 7, 1960, Jim Conner queried Alvin Tilley:

Mr. Bjornlie at Douglas Aircraft called to ask if it [*The Measure of Man*] was available (I told him yes!) He asked if the source or sources from which all this data was gathered had been noted.

In checking I could find no specific reference to any source. The bibliography does not say that these sources were used or to what extent, and incidentally for the male measurements only "armed forces studies" are noted. Does this mean that our 2½ to 97½ percentile men are all military? If so, wouldn't this automatically screen out most civilian males — and especially those not meeting military physical qualifications?

Alvin Tilley, human factors analysis for forklift operation, c. 1957. Tilley's anthropometric charts not only helped designers shape better tools but also served to promote business for the firm. The aura of precision they supplied belied the fact that they were, in the final analysis, his personal interpretation.

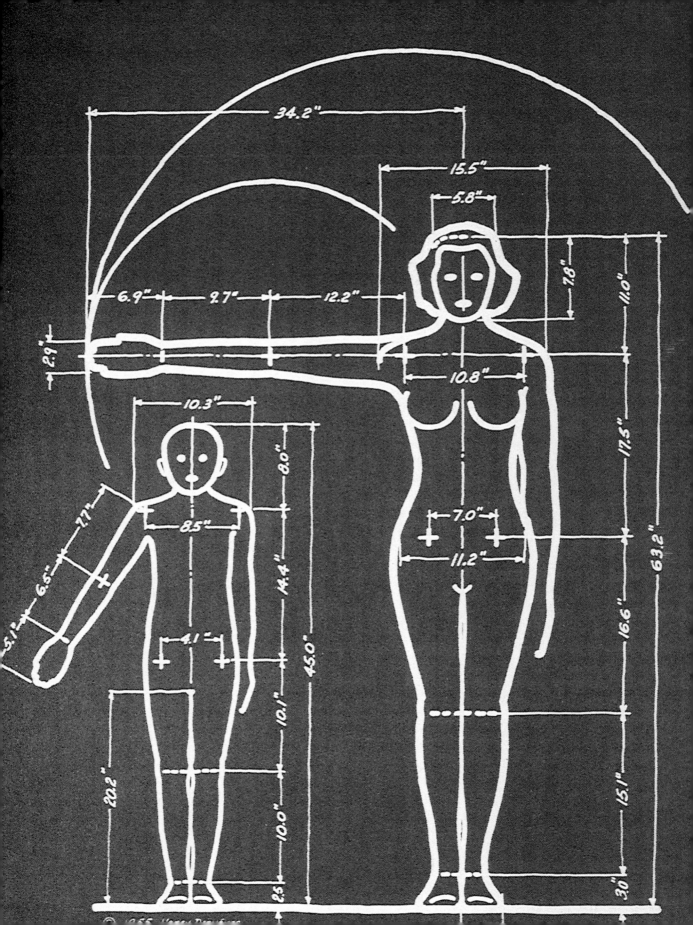

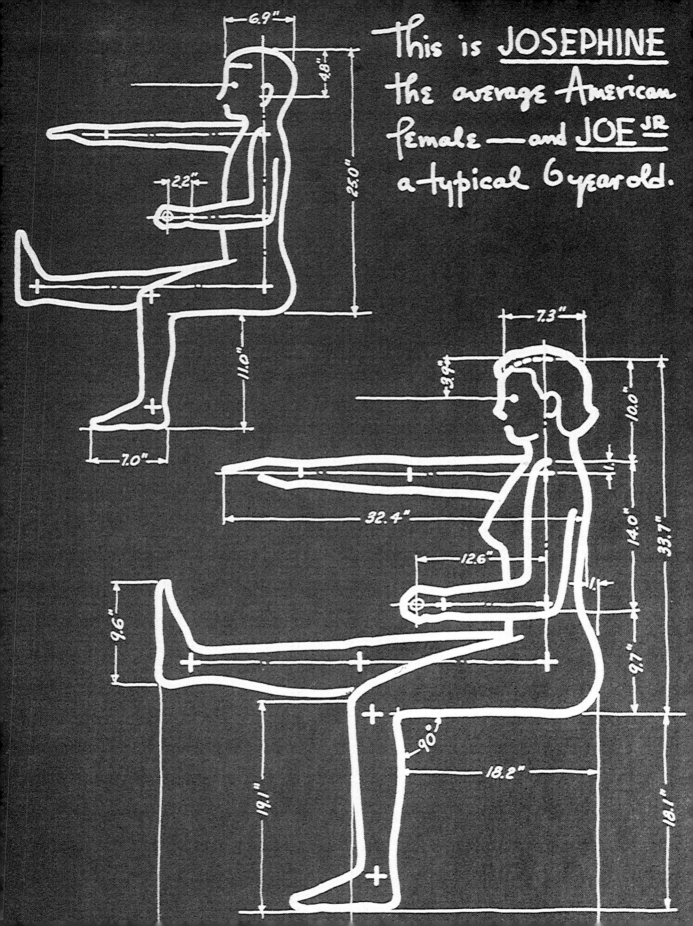

This is JOSEPHINE the average American female — and JOE JR. a typical 6 year old.

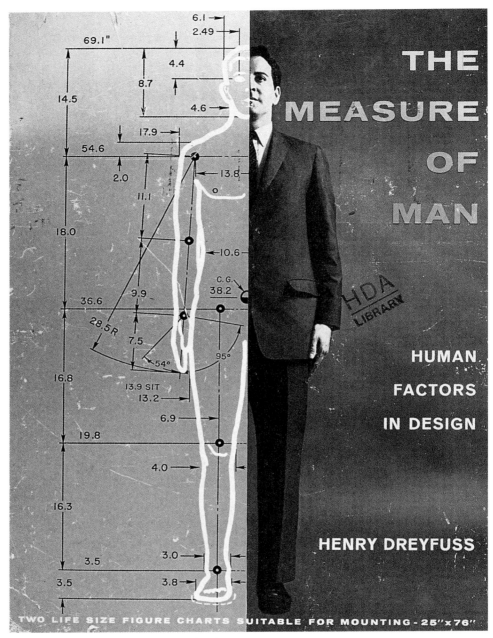

Previous page: Endpapers from the first edition of *Designing for People*, 1955.

Above: cover, *The Measure of Man: Human Factors in Design*, 1960. Dreyfuss had published the first human factors charts drawn by design engineer Alvin Tilley in *Designing for People* in 1955. His 1960 publication was far more comprehensive. It included a life-size chart of Joe as well as numerous other analyses of human anthropometrics, providing other designers with a readily accessible tool kit for framing their own work. Revised in 1967, the book was succeeded by the *Humanscale* series in the 1980s and *The Measure of Man and Woman* in 1993.

The question of source of data will probably be asked again more than once and it might be a good idea to have a well thought out answer to it when the occasion demands.[18]

On the surviving copy of the memo, Doris Marks's penciled notes question whether listing such sources wouldn't prove entirely impractical, making us aware that she did in fact monitor more than just the business aspects of the office's work. Tilley replied to Conner two days later:

Our information is a summation of practical data for our type of use. Some material is a composite of many different sources, some information is extrapolated. If reference sources were given for each piece of data the book would become so voluminous and complex as to be impractical; also we might receive criticism for taking material out of context. (We can give a specific reference source when ever you need it.)

Your point is well taken about the $2^1/_2$ and $97^1/_2$ percentiles not representing the civilian male population. However we are forced to make use of available sources representing the largest number of measurements with wide distributions. We are probably safe for the $97^1/_2$ figure since "military rejection for extremes of height alone accounted for only a negligible small proportion of total rejections" — quote from the Report No. 1 – BM On Men Inducted Into the Army and for Rejected Men during 1943. "Specific causes for rejection relative to height and weight were dwarfism, giantism, disfigurement, pituitary dysfunction, excessive overweight and serious organic diseases." 0.2% rejected for undersize. Size accuracy is more important for the large man, the small man can adjust to improve his position.

Some day better data will be available. Until then we must make use of the tools we now have.[19]

Making use of the tools at one's disposal is an essential component in defining the industrial designer's job description. Rarely charged with the responsibility of inventing a new way of doing things, industrial designers try to stay well informed regarding the progress of others and to seek ways of employing new discoveries. The achievement of the Dreyfuss firm was not, in fact, a matter of original research, although much had been discovered in consultation with Dr. Janet Travell and other experts, but rather the collation and interpretation of data from disparate sources. Tilley's orientation, from his training as a design engineer, was toward the creation of usable tools that would save time in the generation of new designs, utilizing research that had been undertaken before. He updated his information for Joe and Josephine throughout his career with the office.[20] In a narrowly defined sense, this orientation, which he shared with Henry Dreyfuss, was diametrically opposed to the Bauhaus notion of "starting from zero," or relying solely on the designer's concept.

To understand the growing complexity of the relationship between consultant industrial designers and their clients' personnel that developed in the 1960s, one can

Polaroid Corp., Model J33 Land Camera, 1961. The first Polaroid product with which the Dreyfuss office was involved had an electric eye and sold for under one hundred dollars.

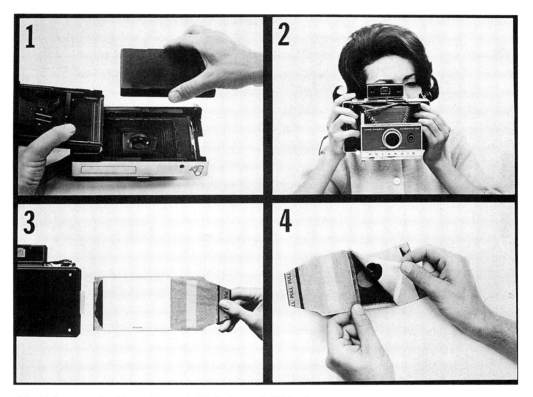

Polaroid Corp., steps in taking a photograph with the Automatic 100 Land Camera, from a press packet of 1963. The introduction of pack film made it possible to operate this camera far more easily than its predecessors. The necessary chemicals were placed in each film packet, which could be removed immediately after a photograph was taken, instead of waiting for the film to develop within the body of the camera.

look to the Dreyfuss office's work with Polaroid Corporation in the 1960s. First it is worth examining Polaroid's orientation toward industrial design, and the history that preceded that relationship.

Edwin Land, founder and presiding genius of this exemplar of technological innovation, had a keen appreciation of the difference that industrial design could make. He had wanted to work with Dreyfuss on the development of his "instant" camera from its inception, but Dreyfuss's commitment to camera manufacturer Ansco prevented him from taking the account.[21] Certainly a recognition of the association between aesthetics and engineering had been involved in the redesign of Polaroid's desk lamp, which was introduced in 1938 and revised in the following year. The first version, a massive-looking structure molded in Bakelite, took its visual cues from a familiar predecessor. It showed an often-encountered tendency in this period to shelter innovation in the garb of the well known — in this case, mounting the polarizing filter that eliminated glare in the body of what appeared to be a banker's desk lamp. When Walter Dorwin Teague was hired to redesign this product, his son Dorwin Teague brought engineering to bear in the creation of the plastic (again, Bakelite) housing that contained the bulb and anchored the Polaroid filter, creating integral vents for cooling in the plastic shell and increasing the effective working area beneath the lamp.[22] A stylish, brushed-aluminum stem that tapered to a Bakelite base was added to the cowl-like shade by Frank Del Giudice. The support looked a great deal like a sculptural exclamation point, emphasizing that this was a very different kind of lamp. In many ways, it is an illustration of the shift from streamlining to "cleanlining" pioneered at the Dreyfuss office during the same period. Examples such as this and Dreyfuss's post-Model 150 vacuum cleaners for Hoover illustrate the evolution of the industrial design aesthetic in the United States, which at its best moved away from simple geometries and teardrop shapes toward more complex, yet defensibly functionalist, forms. Teague's firm would go on to contribute to the first commercially available Land Camera (as the "instant" camera is properly designated), the Model 95, which debuted in 1948.

Dreyfuss's fascination with Polaroid's inventions was continuous in the years up to 1961, when the account was secured. Whether it was "a blaze of Polaroid light" proposed for the Theme Exhibit at the 1939 New York World's Fair or a "curtainless window," obtained by using two Polaroid filters, for Consolidated Vultee's airplanes a little less than a decade later and eventually installed in the portholes of staterooms on the S.S. *Independence*, Dreyfuss sought to apply Land's innovations to his own designs.[23]

The Automatic 100 Land Camera was the first case in which a contribution from Dreyfuss to a Polaroid product had a decisive impact. The breakthrough design made its commercial debut in 1963. According to *Industrial Design* magazine, the new camera was less than half the weight of its predecessors, which brought it into the same range as a number of noninstant, single-lens reflex cameras, then state-of-the-art in 35-mm

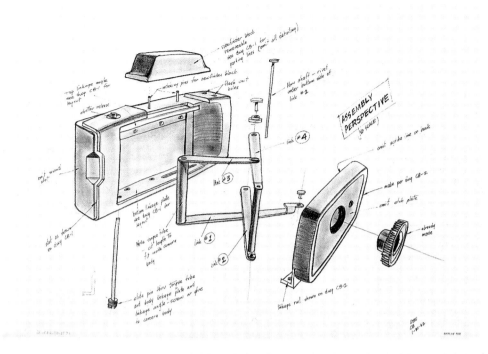

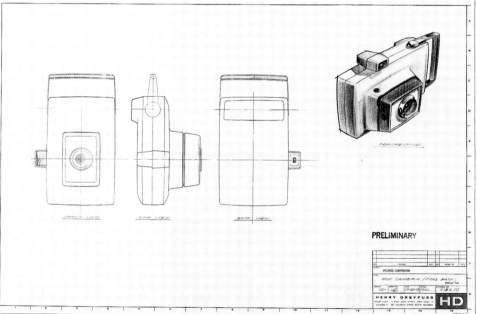

Top: Polaroid Corp., assembly perspective of proposed camera, 1962. The
Dreyfuss firm's involvement with the engineering details of Polaroid's cameras
is indicated by this drawing.

Bottom: Polaroid Corp., preliminary sketch, box camera (roll back), 1963. Seen
in this drawing is a predecessor of the Swinger, the least expensive Polaroid
camera ever marketed.

photography. Perhaps more revolutionary was automatic electronic control of the shutter mechanism, which had been attempted in a previous Polaroid camera but which was considerably refined in this version. The redesign of the mechanism did away with a number of complicated mechanical parts in favor of a greater reliance on electronics. Coupled with an easy-to-use rangefinder, this design reduced the complaints about the cameras producing over- or underexposed and out-of-focus images.

The most significant advance, however, was in the overall operation of the camera. The Automatic 100 introduced pack film — that is, snap-in packages of either black-and-white or color film that eliminated the awkwardness associated with roll films. Roll film had limited the speed of operation and often proved messy in less-than-ideal operating situations. Now users no longer had to wait for the image to develop within the camera body, but could remove the developing photograph and immediately shoot another. Chemicals for each photograph were sealed within discrete packets on the film, eliminating or reducing leakage.[24] This, combined with the introduction of color film that developed in fifty seconds and a new and faster black-and-white film that developed in ten, meant that Polaroid's equipment could successfully compete with that of conventional camera manufacturers.[25]

The Dreyfuss team was headed by Jim Conner, who supervised the work (which was done in the California office) and acted as the primary contact with Polaroid's research, design, and production engineers.[26] Land had begun development of the Automatic 100 by placing a lens atop a film package and stating that Polaroid's next camera should be no larger than those components, clearly an unrealizable goal but one characteristic of his driving vision of a superior, "absolute one-step photography."[27]

The focus of the Dreyfuss contribution was to enhance the camera's ease of use, making buttons and levers more discernible for novices and deriving shapes for these controls that made them easier to operate. While the technology of the film, optics, and electronics were solely Polaroid's province, Conner and others made significant suggestions regarding the reduction of the camera's size (through the arrangement of components) and making the materials lighter and more robust. They applied the office's own system of symbols to the camera (which had begun in work for Deere & Co. and National Supply Company in the late 1950s). In developing the design of the camera, the team had analyzed the individual steps in its handling through charts of a cartoon-like user (a shorthand Joe) to anticipate details of how a Polaroid camera, which could now be slung over the shoulder, could be used most efficiently. The technical capabilities of this camera were thus reconciled to the way people actually used it. For example, now that the developing photographs could be removed from the camera before they were "done," where were they to be stored if the user wanted to take another photograph? Could the user accomplish this with the camera slung over his or her shoulder? Such niceties might not be anticipated by engineers oriented most strongly toward

Above: Polaroid Corp., Polaroid Land Camera Model 20 (Swinger), 1965.
Aiming to bring Polaroid photography to the masses, the Swinger was marketed
at a mere $19.95. Introduced by one of the splashiest advertising campaigns
Polaroid had ever initiated, it is a hallmark of the 1960s passion for fun, plastic,
and immediate gratification.

Left: Polaroid Corp., promotional mailing featuring the Swinger, 1965.
The Swinger's black-and-white photographs made "instant" photography
easily affordable.

HENRY DREYFUSS

300 COLUMBIA STREET · SOUTH PASADENA, CALIFORNIA 91031 · TELEPHONE (213) 799-7151
NEW YORK OFFICE: 8 WEST 58TH STREET · NEW YORK, NEW YORK 10019 · TELEPHONE (212) 751-8020

This new Polaroid camera -
The SWINGER - took this picture
of itself in 10 seconds!

As Industrial Designers for
Polaroid, we worked with their
engineers in designing this
miracle camera -- and part of
the miracle is that it is priced
under $20.

H. D.

Polaroid Corporation, SX-70 Land camera, 1972. Part of the dilemma of writing an accurate history of design can be seen in an example like this breakthrough "instant" camera. While Dreyfuss's firm was an active participant in the shaping of the final product, the vision was that of Edwin Land. Dreyfuss's personal contribution was in selecting leather samples for the exterior of this luxury item.

technical feasibility and cost reduction, but they were essential in ensuring the success of a consumer product. Here the firm's expertise in user behavior, developed in work such as the NIKE missile system for the United States government (where an operational misstep had far graver implications than a too-dark snapshot), found application in peacetime. The result of this work for Polaroid has been a part of everyday experience for millions over the last twenty years. Most cameras used to make identification cards have been Polaroid products, operated by people not necessarily trained in photography who had to be guided through procedures in a straightforward, intelligible fashion. A mixture of symbols and words made this system effective. Drivers' licenses, for example, have been handed to eager new operators in minutes as a matter of course rather than reaching them in the mail days or weeks later.

The Automatic 100 Land Camera defined the start of a new generation of Polaroid products aimed at a broad consumer market (products for scientific, medical, and other specialized purposes had long formed a major, but less visible, portion of the company's output). In a pattern that would be repeated, a relatively high-priced model would be introduced with a number of startlingly new features. Breakthroughs would begin to appear in more modestly priced cameras in the following years, but the lower-priced version would rarely compete directly with the earlier model. A great deal of the Dreyfuss firm's work involved these designs, standardizing appearances while maintaining a certain "snob appeal" for the top-of-the-line model (again, price differentials were based on functional superiority and not appearance alone). For example, changes might call for replacing leather with a plastic substitute, collapsible bellows with solid bodies, or similar cost-saving strategies. The Swinger was an exception to this general principle of operations. Designed from the start to be a product that would be inexpensive enough for teenagers (and debuting in 1965 at $19.95), the Swinger took Polaroid decisively into the world of popular photography. An improved roll film, which reduced costs, also allowed photographs to develop outside of the camera body. A fixed-focus lens coupled with a solid body and an extremely simple photometer exposure system eliminated many user options but did away with guesswork as well. When looking through the viewfinder, the user simply squeezed the stem of the shutter release and rotated it until the word *yes* became distinguishable. This meant that the exposure would be correct, and the shutter could be activated by pushing down on the same stem. Light, easy to use, and affordable, it was accompanied by an advertising campaign that urged consumers to "meet the Swinger." In many ways, it was a return to the basis of popular photography sketched out by George Eastman with his Brownie at the turn of the century, with one important exception: rather than having to wait to see a snapshot, the photographer's gratification was instant. Brownie owners sent both film and camera back to Rochester for processing and reloading; those purchasing the Swinger could see immediate results.

Polaroid Corp., ID-3 Land identification system, 1969. As with the Big Shot, this
Polaroid project reached completion after Henry Dreyfuss's departure from
the firm he had founded. Nonetheless, it exemplified the priorities he had established over the previous four decades.

Polaroid Corp., Big Shot color portrait camera, 1971. Intended only for portraits, the Big Shot was simplicity itself. The user merely approached or backed away from the subject until two images merged in the viewfinder. As a commercial product it was less successful than hoped, but it became a favorite of artist Andy Warhol.

At first glance, the Swinger seemed no different than many other cameras, except that its body was white instead of the expected black.[28] All of its elements, including the one-piece focusing stem/shutter release, involved the Dreyfuss design team from the start. When handling it, the user became aware of the camera's sculptural form. To accept the roll film, the camera's back was made considerably wider on the right-hand side, which also created a substantial hand grip. Weight was reduced through the use of plastics to the point that the camera could be dangled from a plastic strap (as bikini-clad Ali McGraw did in a television commercial that was part of the advertising campaign).[29] The white plastic body had a black "face" that was enlivened by a metallic Mylar "sandwich" that surrounded the lens.[30] Distinct from most of the Polaroid line, it had an undeniably pop-art appearance.

A large and rather simple wood-and-vinyl model of a camera is preserved today in the Polaroid Corporation Archives in Cambridge, Massachusetts. On Dreyfuss's microfilm is a sketch of a similar design, labeled "Homebody." The Cambridge model is for a bellows-type folding camera. Its large size did not make it very portable; rather it was intended as an easy-to-operate "second" camera for portrait photography. The idea again was Land's, but it began to take shape during a meeting with Dreyfuss.[31] It would be a "stay-at-home" camera that might be stored in a closet or behind the couch. What emerged was the Big Shot, a solid-body camera with an extremely long "barrel" that was an offshoot of the earlier Swinger or Model 20 Land Camera, the least expensive Polaroid camera ever marketed. While not a great commercial success, the Big Shot was immortalized by Andy Warhol, who no doubt admired its convenience, and whose output with this camera was as prodigious as Dreyfuss's with his Minox miniature.[32]

Industrial designers had long been involved in the gray areas that exist between the practices of architecture and product design. Exhibition and interior design had become important elements of Dreyfuss's practice by the mid-1930s. Whether these efforts were ephemeral (such as displays for Plymouth Motor Corporation for the National Auto Show in New York in 1933 and 1934) or durable (the model office built for Western Union in Philadelphia in 1936), they make a point about Dreyfuss's practice that is too often ignored. While most industrial design surveys identified him as a shaper of products, the creation of environments comprised a major component of Dreyfuss's work.

Dreyfuss's aesthetic was subtle. While Raymond Loewy accused him of being color blind regarding the interiors of the 20th Century Limited, Dreyfuss no doubt found Loewy and Paul Philippe Cret's interiors for the Broadway Limited garish. Dreyfuss once reminded Loewy that many passengers travel under duress.[33] In an interview, Strother MacMinn noted that to understand the Dreyfuss aesthetic one has to imagine the interiors of the 20th Century Limited decorated by the stylish outfits and cultivated manners of the people riding it, or dining in the Persian Room at the Plaza Hotel, or

American Export Lines, deluxe suite, S.S. *Independence*, 1951. The portholes incorporated two rotating Polaroid filters enabling them to be "dialed" from transparent to opaque. This was part of Dreyfuss's continuing fascination with Land's discoveries and his incorporation of them in his own designs.

dancing aboard the S.S. *Independence*. As with his product design, people were the focus of Dreyfuss's concern: their comfort, their convenience, their safety, and their "inherent sense of good taste." If he sometimes fell back on the dependable (he was an avid admirer of Americana, such as folk carvings, weathervanes, and the like, and used them in otherwise modern interiors), quality was rarely compromised. In creating a new headquarters building for Bankers Trust Company at 280 Park Avenue (between 48th and 49th Streets) in New York, Henry Dreyfuss received top billing. In a press release from his office, the building was described as "the first structure for which entire design responsibility has been given to an industrial designer — Henry Dreyfuss." Yet, in what might be considered his crowning achievement in this area, compromises played a large role.

The project began with the acquisition of the site in 1958 by Rose Associates from the New York Central Railroad on a ninety-nine-year lease for a fixed sum. During negotiations, Bankers Trust Company became interested in possible tenancy, with the stipulation that certain specifications to the "new" building (which in fact partially reused the framework from an older apartment building on the site) would be theirs to make. Likewise, some aspects of the design and fit-out of the building were to be their prerogative. Luckily, it was "a very happy marriage," characterized by collegial relations, according to Frederick P. Rose, president of Rose Associates. He and Herbert G. Maser, who represented Bankers Trust in the negotiations regarding the building, "wanted something better," and both wanted to employ Henry Dreyfuss on the project, primarily for his taste and his sense of practicality. Since Bankers Trust did not want responsibility for the entire space necessary to make the project financially viable, additional rentable office space was always part of the scheme. The two elements were visually separate: the Bankers Trust offices were housed in the base of the skyscraper, and the rental space placed above, distinguished by the setback in the building's exterior halfway up its height.

Rose recalled that it was "the worst possible place to have a building" in that the building stands where the express and local train tracks merge below street level, creating an intricate web of supports to deal with.[34] The basic problem confronted by any architect working on a Park Avenue site has been the existence of the railroad tracks beneath the street. The tracks inhibit placement of elevators at ground level because elevators need a considerable amount of space for machinery beneath the lowest level reached by an elevator cab. Dreyfuss's solution, a rational one, was to make the public ascend steps in approaching the building, which stands on a "platform" raised three feet above the sidewalk. This solution would probably prove unacceptable today because of the issues involving accessibility. Architect Edward Larrabee Barnes was emphatic in stating that 280 Park Avenue has proved to be as good as or better than any building in this area known for its skyscrapers. Dreyfuss consulted informally with Barnes regard-

Bankers Trust Headquarters Building, 280 Park Avenue, New York, exterior view, 1962. This building lacks the typical "wedding cake" silhouette that character- izes so many of its neighbors. Appropriately, Dreyfuss's most notable contribu- tions are to be found on the interior. Emery Roth & Sons were the architectural firm that brought Dreyfuss's ideas to realization.

ing the setback that the building takes as it climbs skyward. Barnes regarded this as a more important challenge than the roofline of the building itself. Dreyfuss created a large, garden-like space at this level (the greenery of the plantings is readily visible from the street level today).[35]

Not everyone was happy with the result. Julian Everett, who in a later interview claimed total credit for the building's interiors and graphics, was convinced that the proportions were seriously marred when the total height of the building was reduced to thirty stories. Everett felt that the building may have been "Dreyfuss's status symbol" but was not proud of the result.[36] Yet critical commentary on the building was generally favorable. "The one strikingly human building on the Avenue," was how *Industrial Design* magazine described it (an exception was made for the "great dignity" of Ludwig Mies van der Rohe's Seagram Building).

> The architecture is not outstanding . . . but it is a building tailored to the bank staff and wealthy clients: not only to shelter them, but to make them comfortable, to reflect their conservative taste, their pride, solidity and hospitality. This unusually resonant expression of a client's personality is partially explained by the fact that the architecture was supervised by an industrial designer — Henry Dreyfuss — and it is the culmination of a corporate identity program.[37]

Architectural Forum noted that few banks had "espoused the visual arts quite as enthusiastically" as Bankers Trust had in their new headquarters.[38]

Betraying Dreyfuss's fascination with mass production, the building was faced in precast, six-by-twelve-foot modules of Mo-Sai, an aggregate of high-strength concrete and translucent quartz. The recessed forms with their intrinsic texture lent the building a visual distinction, a departure from the metal-and-glass ziggurats that surrounded it. Roman travertine was chosen to clad the exterior walls that fell inside the supporting columns and also appears inside in the lobby. At the ground level of the building, visitors encountered two-story screens of woven bronze rods flanking the escalators that lifted them to the elevator banks on the second floor. Sculpted by artist Stephanie Scuris, the screens acted to establish a sense of scale and also partially obscured the bank's vault and first two stories of perimeter offices. Offices on the second level behind the screens were joined by an executive office area overlooking Park Avenue (a row of planters separated the staff's desks from the exterior glass). With the original "garden" of miniature pines and azaleas beneath the escalators in place, the ground level of the building revealed an appreciation of the aesthetic successes of the Seagram Building and the earlier Lever House by Skidmore, Owings and Merrill.

The real impact of Dreyfuss's aesthetic was to be felt on the interior rather than on the exterior of the building. Here Dreyfuss sought to "customize" what might have been a somewhat chilly corporate environment with site-specific artworks. The staff lounge and dining facilities, located on the ninth floor, were enlivened by brighter colors

Julian G. Everett. One of the first designers hired by Henry Dreyfuss, Everett had practiced as an architect until the Depression when he turned to industrial design. Everett's role in the development of the firm's aesthetic was seminal; his influence upon all architectural and interior design projects executed prior to the early 1960s is unquestionable.

Bankers Trust Headquarters Building, 280 Park Avenue, New York, lobby, 1962.
Four escalators carried visitors to and from the first floor of the building.
Plantings softened the regular gridded patterns echoed throughout the building.

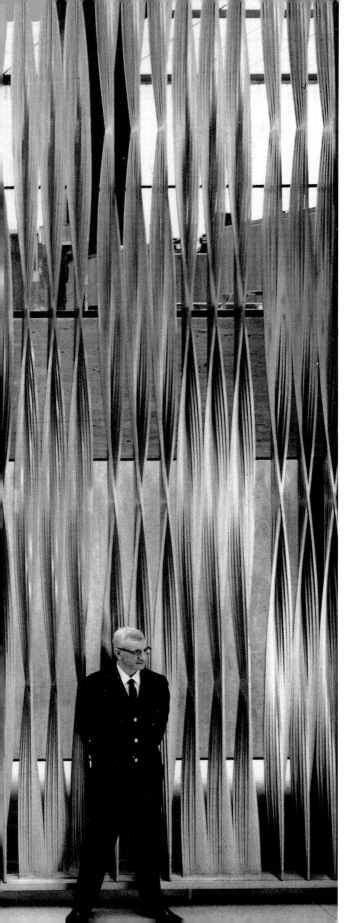

Above: Henry Dreyfuss and Stephanie Scuris inspecting a sample from the sculptor's bronze screen for the Bankers Trust Headquarters, 1962. Perhaps the most striking aspect of Dreyfuss's personal interest in this project was the attention he paid to commissioning artists.

Left: Bankers Trust Headquarters Building, 280 Park Avenue, New York, lobby, sculpted bronze screen by Stephanie Scuris, 1962. Two-stories high, these two massive screens created a visually permeable barrier between public and private spaces in the Bankers Trust lobby and first floor.

Bankers Trust Headquarters Building, 280 Park Avenue, New York, seventeenth-floor reception area, 1962. In the background is Robert Sower's twelve-by-eighteen-foot stained-glass window; its main tonality was a burgundy red.

Bankers Trust Headquarters Building, 280 Park Avenue, New York, wallpiece
for the seventeenth-floor sculpted by Harry Bertoia, 1962. This "sunburst"
sculpture overlooked a staircase that rose from the sixteenth floor. Six and a
half feet across, this magnificent sculpture was welded by Bertoia in his Bally,
Pennsylvania, studio.

Bankers Trust Headquarters Building, 280 Park Avenue, New York, tenth-floor customer dining room, 1962. Dreyfuss selected all of the table furnishings shown. Reproductions of historic tavern signs were mounted on teak walls.

Bankers Trust Headquarters Building, 280 Park Avenue, New York, ninth-floor employees lounge, 1962. Floors were color coded by Dreyfuss and on the ninth floor the accent was red. Dorothy Liebes, a frequent collaborator of Dreyfuss's, designed the custom-woven carpet.

Bankers Trust Headquarters Building, 280 Park Avenue, New York, sixteenth-floor board room, 1962. Typically, Dreyfuss set off this modern interior with art from the past: a seventeenth-century Chinese Coromandel screen in twelve panels.

than seen elsewhere in the building. Accents in red were found in a custom-woven car-pet by textile artist Dorothy Liebes and handwoven screens by Lozano Fischer. The regular grid of the building gave way to a soft curvilinearity in the Liebes carpet and the sofas in the lounge. On the tenth floor, a stained-glass screen in blue tones by Alistair Bevington separated the customer reception and dining areas (Dreyfuss had chosen historic tavern signs to decorate the teak walls of the latter, as well as specifying the table settings, glassware, and linens).

The sixteenth-floor boardroom was decorated with a seventeenth-century Chinese Coromandel screen, and nearby the money room had a complementary eighteenth-century Japanese screen in watercolor on paper. From that level, the bank's officers and their guests ascended a central bronze staircase, where they encountered a re-markable gilded-wire wallpiece created by sculptor and designer Harry Bertoia.[39] A twelve-by-eighteen-foot stained-glass window was fashioned by artist Robert Sowers to separate the executive dining room from the reception area. Two interior garden spaces beneath skylights continued a theme of greenery from the beginning of the building's property line.

Dreyfuss took a tremendous personal interest in the project. Clifford Goldsmith, chairman of Philip Morris when he knew Dreyfuss, recalled that he visited the building one night with Dreyfuss after they had attended the theater; according to Goldsmith, Dreyfuss "knew where every light switch in the place was located."[40] It is interesting to note that when a brochure was printed describing the building's progress at the end of 1962, the cover consisted of a series of printed color "swatches" — some of which had been part of Dreyfuss's aesthetic since the 1930s. Blues and beiges that could have been found on the 20th Century Limited were still a part of his palette.

In 1967, the firm that had been known simply as Henry Dreyfuss became Henry Dreyfuss and Associates. To most observers this would have indicated only that Drey-fuss had decided finally to elevate a handful of his colleagues to a status just below his own; few would have predicted that the founder would leave the firm in less than two years. No one has intimated that a single event or concern lay behind his decision, but it was certainly one he would not have made without consulting Doris Marks.

Dreyfuss left the firm officially on January 1, 1969. He intended to pursue a new career as a corporate adviser after that date. But, according to Bill Purcell, Dreyfuss may not have realized what an effective team he had built. Dreyfuss and Purcell vis-ited major clients together to present Dreyfuss's scheme that both he and his successor firm should continue working for them, although in different capacities. One day, at a meeting in New Jersey with Bell Telephone Laboratories, Dreyfuss encountered little enthusiasm for his plan: "We went to all the clients. AT&T, that didn't work at all. AT&T said, 'No, we think Bill's great. We don't think you ought to stay on.' They said it just like that."[41]

Purcell made a common mistake in relating this story: Dreyfuss actually did continue to advise AT&T, but not Bell Telephone Laboratories, the client for whom the industrial design work was done. That must have been a heavy blow for a man who had begun consulting with them in 1930. (Perhaps this was softened somewhat when he became the first honorary member of the Telephone Pioneers of America in 1971.)

Others did in fact find Dreyfuss irreplaceable: Deere & Co. and Hallmark continued to make considerable use of his talents. Association with Hallmark founder Joyce Hall had begun in the late 1930s, when Dreyfuss persuaded the greeting card company to shelve plans for a World's Fair exhibit in favor of a store on New York's Fifth Avenue. While the Dreyfuss office never officially worked for Hallmark, Dreyfuss himself maintained a steady back-and-forth with Hall and his employees. According to Stanley Marcus, Hall was prone to calling Dreyfuss in the middle of the night to discuss matters. John Dreyfuss recalled his father stopping their car by the roadside one day to pick flowers, not out of a sudden whim to commune with nature, but to send them off as color samples to Hallmark.

The dominant project following Dreyfuss's "retirement," however, had nothing to do with former clients. It had everything to do with the remarkable abilities of Henry Dreyfuss and Doris Marks to gather, collate, and assemble information into a usable form. Together they worked on the *Symbol Sourcebook: An Authorative Guide to International Graphic Symbols*, published in 1972. Its origins lay in the 1950s, when National Supply Company, a manufacturer of oil-drilling equipment, was searching for a solution to the very real problem of seeing their equipment safely operated in regions where English was uncommon. These "pictographs," as they were labeled by Alvin Tilley, sought to use simple, two-dimensional illustrations to "jump the language barrier." There were some false starts: a tortoise was almost universally understood as "slow," but a speeding bullet was tranformed into a running hare to represent "fast."

By the inception of the project, the Dreyfuss firm had been using such symbols for years in conjunction with work for Polaroid, Deere & Co., and others. (Bill Hewitt recalled that French insistence on labels in French frustrated Deere & Co.'s effort to make this a truly comprehensive effort.) In much the same way as Tilley's initial human factors "mural" (showing Joe standing, sitting, driving a vehicle, etc.) provided a "sticking place" for the addition of information on anthropometrics, these early product labels soon began to reach into more challenging areas. Henry Dreyfuss and Doris Marks, along with assistant and consultant Paul Clifton, began to sift through materials received after a mass mailing to professional organizations and friends. The challenge was not simply to put all of this information together but to make it graphically cohesive as well: to simply publish the existing information would only leave the job to someone else. Dreyfuss drew upon a lifelong interest in typography and practical experience that reached back to his revision of *McCall's* magazine in the 1930s. Doris Marks

Henry Dreyfuss planning his *Symbol Sourcebook: An Authoritative Guide to International Graphic Symbols*. Dreyfuss Collection.

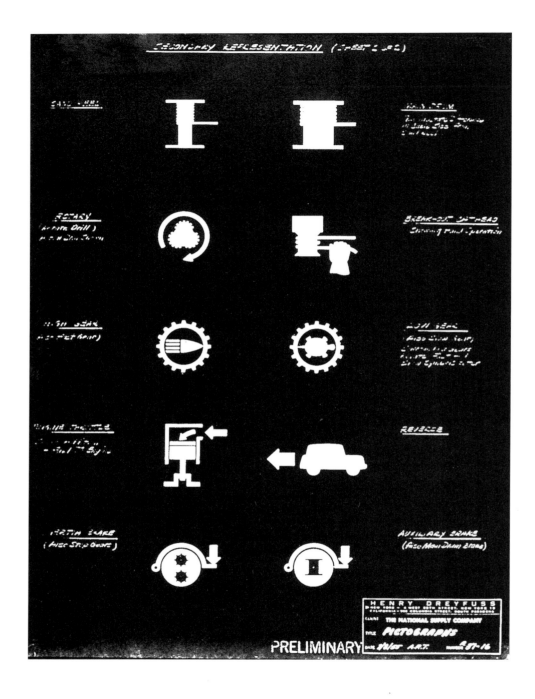

Above: Dreyfuss is shown here in 1972 sketching his shorthand rendition of Leonardo da Vinci's famous illustration of human proportions. This sketch appears on the title page of the *Symbol Sourcebook*.

Left: Alvin Tilley for Henry Dreyfuss, National Supply Co., pictographs, 1955. These earliest surviving symbol studies show the beginnings of Henry Dreyfuss's *Symbol Sourcebook*. Note, in the middle column of the page, the speeding rocket indicates fast and the tortoise slow. A running hare later replaced the rocket for greater "legibility."

Doris Marks and Henry Dreyfuss, 1972, during the completion of the *Symbol Sourcebook*. This project was their final one in a collaboration that had spanned forty-two years, two offices, and three children.

marshalled her expertise in record-keeping and information retrieval. So impressive was the final product that Buckminster Fuller, writing the foreword to the volume, stated openly that he had little use for most industrial designers but that Henry Drey-fuss was an exception. Quickly leafing through the book, one page jumps out at the reader because it lacks the standardization found on all other pages and strikes one as unmistakably Dreyfuss's inclusion: it is a page of symbols as drawn by hoboes, left in the scrawl that would characterize chalk or pencil marks.

At some point in 1972 Doris Marks was diagnosed with cancer of the liver. She evidently decided against any course of treatment that would prolong her life, as recovery from the illness was out of the question. Apparently she and Dreyfuss, who at sixty-eight was still healthy and vigorous, had decided after the initial diagnosis that they would end their lives together when her pain became unbearable. On October 5, 1972, they were found in their car at their South Pasadena home, having succumbed to carbon monoxide poisoning.[42]

Some friends were shocked by the news; others had intuited that their last visit or conversation with Dreyfuss would be, in fact, their last. Perhaps this troubling end to a life that had seemed a definitive success story muffled the acclaim one might expect upon the passing of such a man. Nonetheless, Henry Dreyfuss was recalled in memorial services in both New York and California as a warm and often inspirational figure. The Dreyfusses' quiet generosity to many people emerged with time. For all of his public exposure, Henry Dreyfuss had managed to keep many things private.

This is not the book to discuss the legacy of Henry Dreyfuss; that will be for others who are more knowledgeable about the actual practice of industrial design to do. One aspect of what he left behind, however, seems clear: human values have a place in the shaping of our environment, right down to the tools we grip in our hands. Only when people become the focus of design can we say that we are on the way to fulfilling a promise that Henry Dreyfuss felt was worth keeping.

Notes

1. Dreyfuss, *Industrial Design: Volume 5* (New York: Comet Press, privately printed, 1965?), frontispiece.

2. Dreyfuss, *Industrial Design: A Pictorial Accounting, 1929–1957* (New York: Photogravure and Color Company, privately printed), frontispiece.

3. Dreyfuss, "Products Yet to Come," lecture to the Annual Meeting of the American Association of Advertising Agencies, New York, unpaginated printed transcript in Dreyfuss Collection.

4. "The New Society: Statement by Henry Dreyfuss, President, On the Formation of the Industrial Designers Society of America," *IDSA Design Notes* 1 (April 1965), 2.

5. Ralph Caplan, *By Design: Why There Are No Locks on the Bathroom Doors in the Hotel Louis XIV and Other Object Lessons* (New York, McGraw-Hill Book Company, 1984), 25–26. The phrase "dean of American designers" seems to have first been applied to Norman Bel Geddes, in an article noting that Dreyfuss was the youngest member of this new profession. Carlton Atherton, "Henry Dreyfuss: Designer," *Design* 36 (January 1935), 4.

6. "...the Society of Industrial Designers (SID) was established in 1944 in New York City after the courts ruled in a 1941 Unincorporated business tax suit versus Walter Dorwin Teague (who was supported by other prominent industrial designers) that Teague's primary activity was providing a service to the public and that, therefore, he was not liable for the tax. This has been taken since then as prima facie evidence that industrial designers are professionals." Arthur Pulos, *American Design Ethic: A History of Industrial Design to 1940* (Cambridge, Mass.: MIT Press, 1983), 402.

7. Niels Diffrient, interview with author, March 1, 1991.

8. Ibid.

9. This inscription appears on the exterior of the building that houses the Society for Ethical Culture in New York.

10. Mildred Constantine, s.v. "Dreyfuss, Henry," in *Contemporary Designers*, [Ann Lee Morgan, ed.] (Detroit: Gale Research Company, 1984), 163.

11. Dreyfuss, *Symbol Sourcebook: An Authorative Guide to International Graphic Symbols* (New York: McGraw-Hill, 1972).

12. Terrence Riley and Edward Eigen, "Between the Museum and the Marketplace: Selling Good Design," *Studies in Modern Art* 4 (1994), 164. The artists and designers mentioned are Arne Jacobsen, Kaj Franck, Finn Juhl, Boris Kroll, Marianne Strengell, Freda Diamond, Eszter Haraszty, Trudi and Harold Sitterle, Russel Wright, and Eva Zeisel.

13. Russel Wright and Henry Dreyfuss shared 1904 as their birth year. Charles Eames, born in 1907, had a different sensibility than the industrial designers who founded the SID and represented the next generation.

14. Dreyfuss, *Designing for People* (New York: Simon and Schuster, 1955), 209. Mildred Constantine, who worked in the Department of Architecture and Design, confirmed that the unspecified museum in Dreyfuss's account of this incident was in fact the Museum of Modern Art. Mildred Constantine, interview with author, February 26, 1991. It is interesting to contrast Dreyfuss's anecdote with one found in an early draft of his autobiography: "When the model of a new alarm clock we had designed was presented for final inspection, I appalled our client when I requested that a narrow chromium band be placed around the otherwise simple and functional base. They reminded me that for years I had been the exponent of no extraneous decoration. Eventually they were convinced that I was not expressing my personal taste, but my belief of what the consumer was ready to accept, and that the shiny metal I was recommending would be inoffensive and make the severity of the form acceptable because it would recall other things with which the public was familiar." Dreyfuss, "Book on Industrial Design 1946," *Designing for People* misc. file, Dreyfuss Collection.

15. Charles W. Pelly, interview with author, November 21, 1990. Pelly is the founder and president of Designworks/USA, a California-based design firm that maintains an office in Troy, Michigan, as well. Pelly was president of the IDSA in 1991–92.

16. One person working for the power industry stated that Henry Dreyfuss's handsome fee would still be less than properly burying a single mile of 230 kv power lines. Eugene Levy, "The Aesthetics of Power: High Voltage Transmission Systems and the American Landscape," unpublished paper, History Department, Carnegie Mellon University, Pittsburgh, March 18, 1996, 18.

17. "On the basis of exhaustive medical and human engineering studies, Mr. Dreyfuss has assembled a basic list of human requirements which provides a universal yardstick of good seating design." The phrase appears in an article detailing the creation of a new seat design for Lockheed's JetStar airplane. Norman M. Lloyd, "Comfort Criteria for Seat Design: Dreyfuss-Designed Armchair Provides Universal Yardstick for Passenger Comfort," *Automotive Industries* 123 (November 1, 1960), 44.

18. Jim Conner to Alvin R. Tilley, December 7, 1960, *Measure of Man* Correspondence File, 1973.15.9, Dreyfuss Collection.

19. Tilley to Conner, December 9, 1960, ibid.

20. A revised edition of *The Measure of Man* was issued in 1967, and, with Niels Diffrient, Tilley created the *Humanscale* series. *The Measure of Man and Woman* was nearing completion when he died in 1994.

21. Ansco was owned by film manufacturer Agfa; Dreyfuss had held the account since 1939 and designed a popular, twin-lens reflex camera for Ansco in 1946. Jim Conner, telephone interview with author, August 30, 1996.

22. "The trouble with most desk lamps is that they provide a small pool of bright illumination right under the shade, which rapidly fades out into darkness as the distance from the lamp increases. The user must work in this small area if he needs illumination for his work. The ideal reflector is one which provides the most even amount of illumination all over the desk top.

"This was my goal when I designed the shade for the Polaroid lamp. I assumed that the light came from a point source at the center of the bulb at a height of about 13″ and that it was equal in all directions. As in all reflectors, the angle of incidence equals the angle of reflection, so I drew a curve representing a section of the reflector which reflected each segment of light to an equal space on the surface of the desk. Of course the light source is not a point but a $2^1/_2$″ sphere so the result is only an approximation, but even so it is vastly more even than what you get with a conical shade. I designed the shade with two ridges which are pierced with slots for ventilation.

"Once I had the dimensions and exact contour of the shade I turned it over to Frank Del Giudice, who designed the conical support and the spherical section base for a very simple and effective ensemble." Dorwin Teague, letter to author, July 4, 1993. For illustrations of the two lamps, see "Light Without Glare — Redesigned," clipping from *Modern Plastics* (February 1940). They are also illustrated under the years 1938 and 1939, respectively, in Richard Saul Wurman, *Polaroid* (New York: Access Press, Ltd., 1989), n.p.

23. The effect Dreyfuss sought to achieve must have been aborted late in the formulation of the Theme Exhibit, as the phrase "blaze of Polaroid light" appears in the description of its contents in Frank Monaghan, *Official Souvenir Book: New York World's Fair 1939* (New York: Exposition Publications, Inc., 1939), n.p.; Helen A. Harrison points out the gap between the exhibit as imagined and as realized in "The Fair Perceived: Color and Light as Elements in Design and Planning," in Harrison, ed., *Dawn of a New Day: The New York World's Fair, 1939/40* (New York: Queens Museum/New York University Press, 1980), 50; "Curtainless Window," Davenport (Iowa) *Democrat*, January 26, 1947 (clipping in Henry Dreyfuss file, Deere & Co. Archives, East Moline, Illinois). According to Jim Conner, it was Land who approached Dreyfuss again in 1961. Conner, interview with author, August 30, 1996.

24. Edward Carpenter, "Developing the Product 2: Polaroid Camera," *Industrial Design* 10 (November 1963), 67–71.

25. The Automatic 100 allowed owners the option of using either film.

26. Conner's personal interest in photography also led to his work with Honeywell's Heiland division on the development of electronic flash units for conventional cameras. William F. H. Purcell, interview with author, March 16–17, 1991.

27. Carpenter, "Developing the Product," 69. An illustration of the consistency of Land's vision over the course of some twenty-five years, "SX-70" was the designation of his "dream camera" of 1943 as well as the actual product of 1972. Mark Olshaker wrote of Land, "His original instructions to his engineers [for what became the realized SX-70] consisted of a small list typed triple-space on a single sheet of paper: Compact, Integral, Single-Lens Reflex, Garbage-Free." Olshaker, *The Instant Image: Edwin Land the Polaroid Experience* (New York: Stein and Day, 1978), 172. Jim Conner related in an interview that the single-lens reflex idea was a late development in the program. Conner, interview with author, August 30, 1996. While there were a number of "teething problems" with the new camera, the SX-70 was a crowning achievement that may well have been the most ambitious, successful development program in the Polaroid Corporation's history. The Dreyfuss team was involved from its beginnings.

28. Conner related that this was Land's idea from the inception of the project, and that a great deal of effort was applied to creating a truly opaque white plastic that wouldn't allow light to reach the film. Jim Conner, interview with author, August 30, 1996.

29. Wurman, "1965," *Polaroid* (n.p.).

30. The metallic Mylar was left off one section of this "face"; the nonmetallized plastic formed the flash lens.

31. According to Jim Conner, "Land liked Henry because Henry didn't know what you couldn't do." Figuring out how to do things was the province of Land and his scientists and Dreyfuss's engineering-oriented designers.

32. Dreyfuss took hundreds of pictures with this "spy camera," as it has been popularly dubbed. "He must have discarded 90 percent of the photographs," stated John Dreyfuss. Many were used as a basis for the "travelogues" he illustrated in colored pencil of family vacations, such

as the inaugural voyage of the S.S. *Independence*. John Dreyfuss, interview with author, November 23, 1990.

33. For Loewy's comment, see the issue of *The Keystone* devoted to his work for the Pennsylvania Railroad. Anita A. Pins, "The Pennsylvania Railroad Streamlined by Raymond Loewy," *The Keystone* (official publication of the Pennsylvania Railroad Technical and Historical Society) 24 (Spring 1991), 30, footnote 16. Arthur Detmers Dubin, recognized expert on the train, received the following in a letter from Dreyfuss. "Colors used in transportation should give the passenger a feeling of security. While colors can be bright and cheerful, one must remember that among the passengers some would be going on a vacation, or a honeymoon, but others could be ill or en route to the funeral of a loved one. The Century had a neutral background as a basis for the colors used as accents in the decoration." Dubin to Charles Blardone, December 4, 1991. Blardone published Dubin's refutation of Loewy's accusation in the next issue of *The Keystone*.

34. Frederick P. Rose, interview with author, February 10, 1993.

35. Edward Larrabee Barnes, telephone interview with author, February 5, 1991.

36. Julian G. Everett, interview with Raymond Spilman, 1978; information via a telephone interview between Spilman and author, March 27, 1992.

37. Maude Dorr, "Banker's Trust, Park Avenue: A Designer's Experiment in Architecture," *Industrial Design* 10 (March 1963), 52.

38. "A New Art of Banking," *Architectural Forum* 118 (April 1963), 106.

39. Dreyfuss must have become aware of Bertoia's talents by the time they both worked on the Manufacturers Hanover Bank at 43rd Street and Fifth Avenue in the early 1950s. Architect Gordon Bunshaft headed the project for Skidmore, Owings and Merrill, and Dreyfuss's associate Julian Everett contributed a remarkable round vault door for Mosler Safe that was visible through glass at the street level. Bertoia created a wire sculpture that hung above the escalator that took the public to the banking floor on the second level (the piece created for the Bankers Trust building resembled this sculpture). Equally important was Bertoia's seventy-foot-long bronze-and-steel screen that separated public from private banking areas on the second floor; this may well have been an inspiration for the functional considerations behind Dreyfuss and Scuris's screen at Bankers Trust.

40. "He was a conceited guy — he'd let you know that he thought he was very good," stated Goldsmith, who added that Dreyfuss was the only person he knew from business with whom he would go to the theater or even have lunch. "He never wanted to be huge, and wanted to do no more work than he could do well." Clifford Goldsmith, interview with author, January 14, 1991.

41. William F. H. Purcell, interview with author, March 16–17, 1991.

42. With typical thoroughness, Dreyfuss had left a note for their housekeeper to call their doctor, and another note for the doctor asking him to summon an ambulance.

The 500 series wall telephone for Bell Telephone Laboratories, 1956.

CLIENT LIST 1929-1972

This list is not all-inclusive; it is based on Henry Dreyfuss's yearly records, now in the Dreyfuss Collection. The reader should keep in mind that corporate names changed over the years, and the Dreyfuss firm worked for different divisions of various companies at different times.

AT&T (1938, 1940, 1960–64, 1968, 1972)
World's Fair exhibit interior (see also Bell Telephone Laboratories, Inc.)
Addressograph-Multigraph (1931)
Machines and labels
Aerojet-General Corp. (1961-65)
General Tire logo, graphics program
Agfa Ansco Co. [later Ansco] (1939–46)
Cameras
Air Reduction (1943–44)
Welding equipment
S. L. Allen & Co. (1930)
Garden tools
Alliance Machine Co. (1955)
Cranes
American Airlines (1963–68)
Jet interiors, offices, graphics
American Bus Lines (1946)
Transcontinental bus and accessories
American Chicle (1937, 1941, 1943)
Electric sign consultation, packaging, displays
American Cyanamid Co. (1930)
Lampshades, cups, containers
American Export Airlines (1939–42)
Consultant
American Export Lines, Inc. (1939–57)
Ship interiors, transport planes, passenger liners
American Machine & Foundry Co. (AMF) (1949, 1951–53, 1956–62)
Tobacco machinery, bowling alley equipment, home workshop tools, bicycles, bread wrapping machine
American Piano Co. (1929)
Line of pianos
American Safety Razor Co. (1930, 1960–68)
Razor blade dispensers, packaging

American Seating Co. (1930)
School desk and chair sets
American Stove Co. (1930–32)
Gas stove line
American Thermos Bottle (1936)
Thermos bottle and jug set
Amplexical Corp. (1947)
Cameras
Ansco (*see* Agfa Ansco Co.)
Apex Electrical Manufacturing (1938)
Washing machines
Arnot & Co. (1952)
Office furnishing line
Atchison, Topeka & Santa Fe Railway System (1946–47)
Dining cars
Aviation Corp. (1930)
Trademark for American Airways

BMO Corp. (Lou Brecker) (1936)
International Casino consultation
B.V.D. (1937)
Showroom
L. Bamberger (1930)
Display windows, monograms
Bank of America (1947)
Model bank
Bankers Trust Co. (1958–64)
Exterior and interior design, headquarters building, logo
Bastian Brothers (1931)
Rings
Bausch & Lomb Optical Co. (1959–60)
Slide projectors, ophthalmic instruments, magnifying glasses
Don Baxter, Inc. (1951)
Labels, packaging
Bell Telephone Laboratories, Inc. (1930–68)
Telephones, phone booths, control centers, military projects
Bethlehem Steel Co. (1956–57)
Passenger accommodations on cargo vessels
Bevin Brothers (1936)
Bells
Biltmore Hotel (1931)
Bandstand
Birtman Electric Co. (1930, 1932)
Waffle irons, toasters
Budd Manufacturing Co. (1941)
Missouri-Pacific car

Burroughs Corp. (*see* Todd Co.)
Brown Instrument (1937–38)
Entire line of gauges
Byron Jackson Co. (1948–50)
Pumps, oil-well tools

California Bank
(see United California Bank)
California Fruit Growers (1948)
Juicer
Capstan Glass Co. (1929, 1932)
Glass containers
Carrier Corp. (1944)
Room air conditioners
Chicago World's Fair (1930)
Consultant
Chrysler Corp. (1936, 1939–40, 1954–56)
Showroom consultation, military project
Cities Service Petroleum, Inc. (1934, 1936, 1951–62)
Service stations, signs, executive plane, etc.
Cohn Rosenberger (1930)
Jewelry
Consolidated Vultee Aircraft Corp. (CVAC) (1943–48)
Model 37 and 39 planes, prefabricated house, Convair Car
Copeland Products (1929)
Refrigerator
P. & F. Corbin (1929–32)
Hardware and keys
Corning Glass (1929–30)
Flower show exhibition
Crane Co. (1935, 1940–59)
Bathroom fixture line, plumbing, valves, etc.; in charge of all equipment as of 1940
Curtiss-Wright (1930)
Keystone "Commuter" airplane

Dahlstrom (1930)
Elevator door
Datamatic (1937–44)
800 machine
Deere & Co. (1937–68)
Tractors, farm machinery, graphics, etc.
Delman Shoe Co. (1929)
Displays, shoe designs
Dennison Manufacturing (1929–31)
Displays, showroom, products

Dexter Manufacturing Co. (1930)
Washing machines
Diehl Manufacturing [div.of Singer]
(1962–63)
Vacuum cleaners, floor polishers
Doughnut Corp. of America (1935, 1940)
Doughnut-making machine
DuGrenier (1939)
Cigarette vending machine
Allen B. Du Mont Laboratories, Inc. (1955)
Cathode ray oscillograph

Edison Electric Institute (1966–68)
Electric transmission structures
Elgin National Watch (1934)
Watches
Estate Stove Co. (1941)
Gas ranges
Esterbrook Pen Co. (1957–59)
Writing instruments

Fairbanks Morse Co. (1938–43)
Diesel engine, scales
S. W. Farber (1930–31)
Metal dishes, coffee pots, etc.
Federal Motor Truck (1937)
Truck cabs
Federation of Jewish Philanthropy (1948)
Fund-raising exhibition
First National Bank of Oregon
(1961, 1963–64)
Graphics program

GAF Corp. (see Agfa Ansco Corp)
General Controlar Co. (1936)
Telechime
General Electric Co. (1933, 1941, 1948–49)
Refrigerators
General Time Instruments (1933–45)
(*see also* Western Clock Co.)
Clocks, watches, etc.
Al Gersten (1930)
Playing cards (plastic)
B. F. Goodrich Rubber Co. (1933)
Rubber mats
Goodyear Tire & Rubber Co. (1937)
Double Eagle tire
Graflex (1930)
Consultation
Greater Los Angeles Plans (1947–48)
*Consultant on auditorium and opera
house*
Gruen Watch Co. (1930)
Watch boxes

Hallmark Cards, Inc. (1963–72)
*Consultant, architecture, graphics,
interiors*
Hammtronics Systems (1964–65)
Moisture meter
Hayden, Stone & Co. (1963–64)
Trademark and logos
Hayes Spray Gun Co. (1965–66)
Spray guns
Heiland [div. of Minneapolis Honeywell]
(1958)
Strobonar
Heinrich-Lanz [div. of Deere] (1957–60)
Tractors, farm equipment
Herald Tribune (1953)
General design
Hickok Belt Co. (1931)
Buckle designs
Charles F. Higgins & Co. (1932)
Vegetable glue can and trademark
Hilton Hotels (1950)
General design, Persian Room
Hodges Research & Development Co.
(1948)
Meat tenderizer cabinet
R. Hoe & Co., Inc. (1956–59)
Printing presses
Honeywell, Inc. (*see* Minneapolis Honey-
well Regulator Co.)
Hoover Co. (1934–54)
Vacuum cleaners, irons, toasters
Hoover, Ltd. [England] (1950–51, 1957–60)
Washing machine
Howe Folding Furniture Corp. (1931)
Folding chairs
Hudson and Manhattan Railroad
(1949–50)
Train cars, terminals, concession stands
Hughes Tool Co. (1968)
Helicopter interiors
Hygrade Sylvania (1940)
Fluorescent light fixtures
Hyster Co. (1951–68)
Lift trucks

ILG Electric Ventilating Co. (1944)
Fans
E. Ingraham Co. (1949–56)
Clocks, watches

Jacobs Brothers (1930)
Scales

Walter Kidde & Co., Inc. (1955–57)
Fire extinguisher
Kingston-Conley Electric (1948)
Electric motor and grinder

Lane Co. (1929)
Cedar chests
Clarence Lewis (1933)
Office design
Life Magazine (1938)
Consultation, redesign
Liggett & Myers (1930)
Fatima cigarette carton
Lightolier Inc. (1952)
Medicine cabinet
Link Aviation, Inc. (1953–55)
Flight trainers, instruments
Lloyd Sabaudo (1930)
*Transatlantic liner cabins (never
produced)*
Lockheed Aircraft Corp. (1951–64)
*Passenger plane interiors, prefabricated
housing*

R. H. Macy (1929–30)
Windows, exhibits, flower shows
Martin Co. (1961)
Consultant on Apollo project
McCall Corp. (1932–44)
McCall's magazine design
McCallum Hosiery (1930)
Consultant
McCaskey Register Co. (1932)
Vertical register
Mergenthaler Linotype Co. (1948–61)
Linotype machine, office design
Minneapolis Honeywell Regulator Co.
(1934, 1937–38, 1941, 1947–62)
Thermostats, valves, gauges, control panels
Mosler Safe Co. (1952–60)
Vault doors, safes, deposit drops

National Academy of Sciences (1955)
Consultant on human engineering
National Biscuit Corp. (Nabisco) (1940)
Biscuits, packaging, etc.
National Blank Book Co. (1930)
Showroom, trademarks, products
National Dairy (1931)
Packaging design
National Distillers (1937)
World's Fair exhibit
National Research Council (1948–50)
Consultant on artificial limbs

National Supply Co. (1949–58)
  Pumps, oil rigs, etc.
Netherlands Trade Commission (1950)
  Utrecht trade fair exhibit
New York Central System (1936–48)
  *Mercury (1936) and 20th Century
  Limited (1938) trains; railroad equipment
  and consultation*
New York World's Fair, 1939 (1937–39)
  *Exhibit Administration Building,
  Perisphere exhibition*
New York World's Fair, 1964 (1960)
  Design board
Newell Manufacturing Co. (1936)
  Curtain hardware
Nineteen Hundred Corp. (1933)
  Washing machine

Ohio Brass (1953–54)
  High-voltage equipment
Omark Industries, Inc. (1962–67)
  Corporate graphics, tools

Pan American World Airways
(1947–48, 1950, 1953–54)
  Interior of Boeing 377
Park Lane Hotel (1950–51)
  Redesign of lobby floor
Plymouth Motor Corp. (1933–34)
  National Auto Show display
Polaroid Corp. (1960–72)
  Camera equipment, accessories, consultant
Preco, Inc. (1963–64)
  Hair clippers
Price Brothers (1933)
  Displays, signs, stands
Profexray [Division of Litton Industries]
(1966–67)
  X-ray equipment

Radio Corporation of America (RCA)
(1929–30, 1946–55)
  *Radios, phonographs, televisions, air
  conditioners*
Remington Office Machines (1966–68)
  Office equipment
Reader's Digest (1937)
  Magazine format
Rex Cole (1934, 1938)
  Truck, Armonk Room (1938)
RKO Theaters (1929–32)
  Permanent settings, theater renovations
Roseland Dance Hall (1929–40)
  Bandstands, etc.
Royal Typewriter (1936–37, 1944–45)
  Standard and portable typewriters

Sears, Roebuck & Co. (1932–34)
  Washing machine
Sebring Pottery Co. (1930)
  Plates
Seth Thomas Clock Co. (1930–32)
  Clocks, novelties
Singer Co. (1959–68)
  Sewing machine line, special shops
L. C. Smith Typewriter Co. (1930)
  Corona typewriter
Socony Vacuum (1934–37)
  *Rockefeller Center animated display,
  showrooms, travel bureau at 26 Broadway
  (1936)*
Southern California Edison Co. (1962,
1964–67)
  Transmission poles
Southwestern Engineering Co. (1965–66)
  Separators
Speed Products (1939)
  Stapling machine consultation
E. R. Squibb (1929)
  Bottles
Standard Gas Equipment (1929)
  Stove details
Stanley Works (1929)
  Hinges
Statler Hotels [later Hotels Statler Co.,
Inc.] (1938, 1941, 1948–49)
  Room design
Steinway & Sons (1930)
  Line of grand pianos
Swift & Co. (1931)
  Labels

Telautograph Corp. (1955–56)
  Facsimile transmitters
Teletype Corp. (1960–68)
  *Stock exchange ticker, portable teletype-
  writer, tape apparatus, trademark*
Time Magazine (1943)
  Design consultation
Times Facsimile Corp. (1950-59)
  Stencil machine
Todd Co. (1933, 1935, 1939, 1945, 1947)
  Check-writing machines ("Protectograph")
Towle Manufacturing (1930–45)
  Silver display
Tracerlab, Inc. (1950)
  Geiger counter
E. M. Trimble Manufacturing (1929)
  Children's furniture

U. S. Manufacturing Co. (1933, 1935)
  Fly swatters for F. W. Woolworth
United Airlines Transport Co. (1936)
  DC-3 airplane interior, accessories

United California Bank (1957–66)
  Interiors
United Cigar Co. (1938)
  Cigar and drug stores
United States Army (1951)
  *Tank interiors, armored vehicles, rocket
  launchers*
United States Government (1942, 1943,
1954–56)
  *Conference rooms, defense strategy room,
  weapons*
United States Navy (1949–50)
  *DD/927 Class destroyer interiors, AGB/4
  icebreaker*
United States Peace Corps (1961)
  Logo
Uris Hotels (c. 1950–55)
  Room design

William K. Vanderbilt (1936)
  *Private plane (Sikorsky S-43 amphibious)
  interior*

Wadsworth Watch Case Co. (1930)
  Watches
Wahl Co. (1930, 1939–40)
  Pen and pencil set, desk accessories
Warner & Swasey Co. (1939, 1942–68)
  Turret lathes
Washburn Co. (1934–39)
  *Line of kitchen utensils, bathroom
  accessories*
Waste King Corp. (1959–60)
  Appliances
Western Clock Co. (Westclox) (1930–36)
  Clocks, watches, showroom
Western Electric (1943)
  Army and Navy contract work
Western Union (1936)
  *Office design (typical office, Philadelphia,
  1936)*
S. S. White Dental Manufacturing Co.
(1936, 1940, 1954-57, 1962–64)
  Dental equipment, furnishings
Whitman Candies (1929)
  Packaging
Winton Watch Co. (1929)
  Watches

Yawman & Erbe Mfg. (1931)
  Desks, desk details, etc.
Youngstown Pressed Steel (1932)
  Washing machines, color schemes

Model of an alternate-motion wall clock for the Ingraham Company, 1956.

Index

Photographic Acknowledgments
Cooper-Hewitt, National Design Museum Collections:
Applied Arts and Industrial Design Department: 54, 97, 118 (bottom); Drawings
and Prints Department: 26, 34 (top), 53, 109, 110, 111, 114, 121, 140 (middle),
141, 150, 183; Donald Deskey Collection: 90; Dreyfuss Collection: 4, 8, 12, 20, 22,
29, 33, 34 (bottom), 35, 36, 39, 40, 46, 48, 49, 55, 56, 57, 61, 64, 65, 67, 68,
69, 70, 72, 76, 78 (bottom), 80, 81, 82, 83 (top), 85, 86, 89, 91, 92, 94, 95, 98,
101, 115, 119, 122 (top), 123, 124, 125, 126, 127, 128, 129, 131, 132, 133, 135,
142, 147, 166, 168, 170, 172, 173, 175, 176-77, 178, 185, 192, 194-95, 196,
198, 199, 200, 201, 202, 205, 206, 207, 208; Dreyfuss Collection microfilm: 51,
52, 78 (top), 79.

Other Sources and Collections:
Better Homes & Gardens, October 1948: 116; Billy Rose Theatre Collection, New
York Public Library: 28; Eric and Nanette Brill Collection: 71; Deere & Co. Archives,
Moline, Iowa: 120, 148; Henry Dreyfuss Associates, New York: 31, 171 (top); Ethical
Culture/Fieldston School Archives, New York: 24, 25; Paul M. Fitts, ed., *Psychological
Research on Equipment Design*, 1947: 88 (top); Russell Flinchum: 113, 117, 118 (top),
152; *Fortune*, November 1954: 88 (bottom); Rita Hart: 171 (bottom); Honeywell,
Minneapolis: 140, 145; Randy Leffingwell: 149 (bottom), 155; *Life*, 28 October 1945:
83 (bottom); Strother MacMinn: 18, 93 (bottom); Stanley Marcus: 16; New York
Central System Historical Society, Inc.: 6, 58, 59, 60, 62-63, 66; Polaroid Archives,
Cambridge, Massachusetts: 181, 186; Private Collections: 38, 50, 87, 99, 100, 102,
103, 104, 116, 119, 122 (bottom), 134, 136, 137, 140 (top), 144, 149 (top), 151,
154, 157, 159, 180, 188, 189, 190, 193, 197; William F. H. Purcell: 93 (top); John
Waddell Collection: cover, 73, 112.

Photographers:
Apeda Photo Studio, New York: 28; Ruth Bernhard: 50; Dennis Cowley: cover,
34 (top), 71, 73, 97, 109, 110, 111, 112, 118, 121, 141, 150, 183. Mary Frampton:
207; Mel Goodman: 189; Larry Harmon: 172, 173; Dave Henderson: 12; Hans Knopf:
133, 136 (bottom), 137; J. Alex Langley: 199; Randy Leffingwell: 149 (bottom), 155;
Strother MacMinn: 18; Ken Pelka: 54, 123; Robert Yarnall Richie: 192, 194-95, 196,
197, 198, 200, 201, 202; Ezra Stoller: 90.

The following companies supplied photographs and permissions for illustrations in
their archives: AT&T Archives, Warren, New Jersey; Deere & Co. Archives, Moline,
Iowa; Henry Dreyfuss Associates, New York; Honeywell, Minneapolis; Hoover
Company, Canton, Ohio; Polaroid Archives, Cambridge, Massachusetts; U.S. Steel.

Note on the Henry Dreyfuss Collection
Industrial Design Archives, Cooper-Hewitt, National Design Museum

Prior to their deaths in 1972, Henry Dreyfuss and Doris Marks Dreyfuss gave materials they had retained after their 1969 retirement from the firm to the Cooper-Hewitt Museum (they also endowed the Doris and Henry Dreyfuss Memorial Study Center, which is the Museum's library). Materials previously donated to CalTech, the California Institute of Technology in Pasadena (largely Dreyfuss's early theatrical work), were transferred to the Museum in 1973. During this period, former clients were solicited for additional material, which also entered the collection. In 1991 Henry Dreyfuss Associates donated some 400 reels of microfilm records to the collection. These records are copies of materials that were discarded when the office began microfilming its records in 1948, and thus they included work that had been created as early as 1929. At this writing, cataloguing of this material awaits funding.

Researchers interested in the contents of the collection should be aware that the bulk of the collection was published in microfiche form in 1986 by Mindata, Ltd., as *The Henry Dreyfuss Archive*. The one hundred fiches in this publication document biographical files, theatrical design, industrial design, publications by and about Henry Dreyfuss, and include the Research Guide to the Collection.

The Dreyfuss Collection is mainly housed in the Study Center; unique works of art, however, are in the Drawings and Prints Department; and a small number of objects are housed in the Applied Arts and Industrial Design Department.